T H E
ONLY
ONE

ENDORSEMENTS

When talking about missional movement leadership, I have often said that Curtis Sergeant is the best of us all. He has a genius-level intelligence, single-minded focus, authentic humility, and burning passion. The result of this combustible combination is Kingdom movements all over the world. This book may seem simple and basic, but don't let that fool you. What he puts in this small book is actually the key to making disciples worth multiplying. This book is a window into the soul of a world changer, so pay attention.

NEIL COLE
Catalyst for global organic church movements and author of many books, including
Organic Church, *Primal Fire*, and *Rising Tides*

Curtis Sergeant has had more impact on world missions than anyone else I know today. Why? *The Only One* reveals the heart and thinking of a man totally sold out, utterly passionate and consumed with Jesus and His Kingdom. I found myself alternately inspired, convicted, and profoundly challenged. If your longing is to see the expansion of God's Kingdom in the world, I highly recommend not just reading this book, but allowing its principles to change your life.

FELICITY DALE
Author of *An Army of Ordinary People* and coauthor of *Small Is Big!*

Curtis Sergeant has done a wonderful job of assembling practical concepts and tools that will challenge you to put your faith into practice. It will revolutionize your quiet time with the Lord.

PAUL ESHLEMAN
President, Finishing the Task, and former President, Jesus Film Project

I have personally known Curtis Sergeant for many years as a man of great wisdom and deep intellect. Yet it is Curtis's unquenchable desire for himself and others to seek and obey Christ above all else that drives the pulse of this important book. Curtis seeks to compel readers toward completeness in Christ at all costs. Curtis writes with urgency and singularity of focus, as if our lives and their impact on eternity hang in the balance of our understanding of God's design. They do. I would challenge you to approach the content of this book accordingly.

JOHN HEEREMA
Founder and President, Biglife

What a goldmine of biblical truth. It is filled with brilliant and practical insights into increasing your intimacy with God, your unity with God's people, and your impact for God's Kingdom.

DAN HITZHUSEN
Director, Issachar Initiative, and former International Vice President, e3 Partners

The Only One somehow finds the perfect connection between "being" and "doing" for God. I suppose it's because the book's author lives in that intersection. *The Only One* doesn't really focus on explaining how to bring about a disciple-making movement in the tactical sense. But I'm convinced that if more of us could live out the instructions in this book, movements would multiply like crazy. That's because instead of focusing on formulas and quick-fix tactics, this book focuses on how to be a disciple. You will not find a more Bible-based approach. Nor will you ever find an author so humble, so tireless in his chase after Christ, nor so committed to snatching humankind from hell. Here's the bottom line: If you want to be like Jesus, read the Bible—and do this book.

DOUG LUCAS
Founder and President, Team Expansion

Reading and applying *The Only One* will explode in and through your life the joy-filling adventure of knowing and sowing the love of our Father wherever and whenever you go!! Curtis and I have been weeping and reaping as God has woven our lives together in the joy-filling purpose and work of making disciples worth multiplying. As you read, listen, apply, share, journal, calendar, and pray through each chapter of *The Only One*, the Holy Spirit will draw you step by step into living fully in, by, and for God. So as David said to his son Solomon in 1 Chronicles 28:20, I say to you: "Be strong and courageous"— and JUST DO IT!

COLIN MILLAR
prayer igniter at Global Alliance for Saturation Church Planting
and Gospel Media Outreach

Curtis Sergeant has done it again! His take on living fully in, by, and for God will greatly encourage any Christ-follower looking to live with God's eternal Kingdom in mind. Curtis does a great job of offering thoughtful insights that are drawn out of practical experience and personal study deeply anchored in Scripture. This book is incredibly comprehensive, but also very easy to apply to one's life and train others as well. Curtis has been a great source of inspiration to walk closer with Jesus in my own life and the lives of countless others around the world. When you read this book, I expect the same will be true in your life as well. Get ready to listen, apply, and share with others all God is calling you to do and be.

JARED NELMS
Vice President, The Timothy Initiative

In *The Only One*, believers—regardless of location, upbringing, education, or culture— are empowered with encouragement and practical guidance on how to pursue Christ with their whole being. I've had the privilege of co-laboring in Great Commission work with Curtis Sergeant and can attest that the words penned herein are the fruits of his own love for Christ and joyful surrender to His mission. We have much to glean from this passionate brother! The lessons, prayers, and practical tools within these pages are must-reads for anyone desiring to lead a life consumed by fully surrendered devotion to our triune God, who is worthy of all glory and honor and power forever and ever. And thankfully, Curtis has made this inspired new toolbox available to the global body of Christ at no cost! This is a true work of faith and a labor of love!

KURT NELSON
President, East West Ministries

Curtis's humility and depth of insight from a long and close walk with the Lord Jesus are captured here in *The Only One*. Read slowly with your Bible in one hand, as the density of the content is more than you may think at first. You have here a guide to living fully for Jesus. Not a wasted word.

STEVE PARLATO
movement catalyst in Southeast Asia

Curtis expresses a pastor's heart for the individual disciple, a strategist's mind for the need to see biblically healthy churches form and multiply around the world, and a theologian's intelligence to "rightly divide the Word." In combination, this most recent effort provides a pathway for the ardent Christ-follower to discover what our Savior desires for us all: a deeper relationship, which, when sought in fellowship with others, has the potential to truly transform a neighborhood, city, country, or region. Don't just read it. Experience it, walk through it, and see if it will not lead you to honor God as He desires. God not only wants you to know Him, He also wants you to live Him before the world.

DAVID POPE
former Director of the Issachar Initiative and the Global Church Planting Network

Discipleship is not disciplined Bible study, deeper prayer life, faithful worship and witness; these are tools in the process, but discipleship is learning to walk in obedience to God-awareness and understanding that becoming Christlike comes only through self-denial and submission. This book takes readers on a personal pilgrimage of discovering these truths and learning to apply them to lifestyle practices. It is also a great guide for group discipleship of several people who have committed to growing with mutual accountability, or as a resource for someone mentoring others.

JERRY RANKIN
former President, International Mission Board, Southern Baptist Convention

We're living in changing and tumultuous times. Curtis's book is a prophetic word and anchor for the church during these times. It is deeply spiritual and devotional yet enormously practical, written by a practitioner with a global perspective and international experience. A must-read and destined to be a classic.

FRANK SCHATTNER
Jonathan Project International Coordinator, author of *The Wheel Model*

Curtis Sergeant has been a sincere and fruitful follower of the Lord Jesus Christ for decades. He is, without a doubt, one the most successful disciple makers on the planet, having personally catalyzed, or having been partially responsible for, scores of disciple-making movements that span the globe and have resulted in millions of genuine disciples. In this book, his first, he reveals the core secrets of his spiritual fruitfulness. They all revolve around devotion, obedience, and abiding in Christ. All his principles can be imitated by any believer, anywhere, anytime. I can't recommend this book enough. Read it thoughtfully, be challenged, and enjoy greater fruitfulness for the glory of God.

DAVID SERVANT
Founder, Heaven's Family

Curtis lives out the message of this book. His passion for God and for the lost overflows and influences those around him. His training and mentoring help disciples become more faithful and fruitful. God blesses the simple, effective ministry methods that he creates to bring about disciple-making movements in a wide variety of contexts. This book covers both individual and corporate aspects of Theopraxy and also includes proven tools to grow in it. I pray that many will joyfully heed its important message.

ANDY SMITH
International Coordinator for Evangelization, OMF International

Experienced leaders know they can't lead on empty. They also know that being ambassadors for God's shalom requires one to be poured out daily, thereby requiring a constant need to be refreshed. Curtis Sergeant's *The Only One* addresses this by helping one set the metronome of one's heart and life to be in healthy rhythm and reliance on God to serve. More than just a one-time read, this book is a new tool on the dashboard of my life.

NATE VANDER STELT
Executive Vice President, Global Alliance for Church Multiplication

Curtis Sergeant lives as authentically for *The Only One* as anyone I know today. The direction of my life has been radically altered—not by his theory, but by his life. This book is a powerful resource to help us see and experience what it means to live fully in, by, and for our awesome God and King. If you want to know what that looks like, read and apply this book.

TOM VICTOR
President, The Great Commission Coalition

In today's me-centered and ego-driven culture, we desperately need this message. Written by my close friend Curtis Sergeant, *The Only One* brilliantly explains the purpose and power of God-centered thinking and the path to living a God-centered life. Read this book slowly and prayerfully, writing your responses in a journal. Then get a second copy for a friend and reread it, discussing it together. This book is transformational.

RICK WARREN
author of *The Purpose-Driven Life* and Founding Pastor of Saddleback Church

This is a book for dreamers and doers. It is scripturally sound, but not only a book to gain knowledge. It also shares how to be doers in very practical ways, not just hearers of the Word. This book is a fantastic tool that passes on to others the patterns and principles of multiplicative influence from a posture of intimacy and oneness with God and one another. Curtis is not a theoretician, but rather a practitioner of what he has written. Everyone reading and applying what he shares will be blessed and equipped to be both faithful and fruitful for the glory of God.

LEE WOOD
Founder and President, One Body Global

THE
ONLY ONE

LIVING FULLY IN, BY, AND FOR GOD

Curtis Sergeant

WILLIAM CAREY PUBLISHING

Published by William Carey Publishing
10 W. Dry Creek Cir
Littleton, CO 80120 | www.missionbooks.org

William Carey Publishing is a ministry of Frontier Ventures
Pasadena, CA 91104 | www.frontierventures.org

Adazing, cover design
Mike Riester, interior design
Andrew Sloan, copyeditor
Melissa Hicks, managing editor

ISBNs: 978-1-64508-233-0 (paperback), 978-1-64508-235-4 (mobi), 978-1-64508-236-1 (epub)

Printed Worldwide

23 22 21 20 19   1 2 3 4 5   IN

Library of Congress Control Number:2019945985

CONTENTS

Check box **1** when you've **read & processed** the chapter;
2 when you've **applied** the contents to your life;
3 when **you've taught someone** the contents;
4 when that person has begun to **implement** what they've learned;
5 when that person **taught someone else** what you taught them.

WHY I WROTE THIS BOOK

And the LORD will be king over all the earth;
in that day the **LORD** will be *THE ONLY* ONE,
AND HIS NAME *THE ONLY* ONE.
—ZECHARIAH 14:9

I wrote this book to share with you what I have learned about walking with Jesus from decades of pioneering mission work in some of the darkest places on earth. Though the locations were exotic, the principles are universal. They apply to everyone who desires to follow Jesus.

During the first twenty-eight years of my life, I excelled at everything I put my hand to. I was an excellent student and athlete. As a result, I was highly self-confident. And everyone, including me, saw me as a "good Christian" who was working to obey God's Word and expand His Kingdom.

I began focusing on reaching an unreached, unengaged people group (UUPG) in a primitive, isolated, and restrictive environment. One large island had a population of nearly seven million people, but fewer than one hundred known believers. In that context, I discovered that my talents and hard work were not enough. I truly realized, for the first time, that Jesus was absolutely serious when He said, "Apart from Me you can do nothing" (JOHN 15:5B).

I realized my perspective had been exactly upside down. I thought I was at the summit when actually I had never really started to climb. All my efforts and accomplishments were meaningless if they were apart from God's intentions. My own efforts would never accomplish any of God's purposes. The only way I could live the life God intended was to be about His will in His way, in His timing, and by His power.

Living life like this would require a lot more listening and a lot less forging ahead on my own. It would mean more of Him and less of me. Ironically, I had already considered JOHN 3:30 my life verse: "He must increase, but I must decrease." At that point, I began to understand a little of what that verse means.

During the following five years I developed (or gathered from others) the tools and principles contained in this book. I began to experience joy, fulfillment, and an intimate walk with Jesus, and my wife and I began to see fruitfulness in a new way as we labored among the UUPG. By the end of five years I saw fruit that I had only dreamed of as a lifelong aspirational goal. Soon every village among this large people group had a church. These thousands of churches began to serve as a missions force among many other people groups. Disciples made other disciples, down to many spiritual generations. I realized my desires were too weak. My aspirations were too small. God's plans for me were far bigger and better than I would dare to imagine.

I began to invest all my time and energy in equipping others to experience what I had begun to taste. My trainees were, like me, long-term missionaries focused on the spiritually darkest places on the planet. Many saw similar results and experienced similar things. After seven years of training and coaching more than a thousand people through intensive one-month programs, I sensed the Lord calling me to relocate to the United States.

I didn't want to come back to the US. Since my parents were missionaries and I had grown up overseas, this was an unwanted call to a land I did not relate to. I saw it as an inconvenience, because now I would have to travel farther to get to the spiritually darkest places, the places to which I had been called as a high school student. I continued to focus all my attention on what would impact these dark places for the Kingdom of God.

Then, after eleven years of focusing on the most unreached people groups and places in the world while operating from the United States, God clearly showed me that He wanted me to begin to focus half my effort on people in the US. He wanted me to share what I had been sharing in the frontier missions world with believers in this country. He showed me that many American Christians were as blind as I had been for so many years, not knowing that a more abundant life is available to them. They love God and are seeking to serve Him in the best way they know. They are doing what they have been taught and what has been expected of them. This is true for both those in the pews and those in the pulpits. But God has more for us, if we will learn to follow Him fully.

The only reason I saw a deeper way to live out my faith was that God put me in a desperate situation, cut off from any external support system (except for my wife, Debie) and from any distractions. There I was confronted by my own insufficiency and forced to rely only on Him. Without this, I might never have seen another way to live out my faith.

Many North American believers have never had this opportunity. They have ample support systems and unavoidable distractions. There are also obstacles in the form of those who oppose movements in this direction because they feel threatened by the introduction of unfamiliar spiritual expressions and thus discourage anyone who begins to question familiar patterns.

I have now been pursuing this half-time focus on the US for seven years. God is working here just as in frontier mission areas. Every culture has its strengths and weaknesses. Every place has its barriers to the gospel.

I believe the greatest enemy of genuine discipleship in the US is the prevailing paradigm of what it means to follow Jesus. I pray that God will use this book to change that concept. I believe the Lord earnestly desires a radical life for all His children. Speaking about radical Christianity is extremely politically incorrect. Jesus was radical, however, and we are called to walk as He walked (1 JOHN 2:6).

From time to time, I have been asked to endorse books written by others. My policy has been to endorse only books written by successful practitioners, not ivory-tower thinkers. Who would want to read a book on parenting by someone who has never been a parent?

Now, for the first time, I have written my own book. I never aspired to write one. I wrote it because I believe God told me to write it. I suspect that it will be as much for my benefit as for anyone else's. But I feel a bit awkward as I consider my own endorsement criterion. I cannot claim to be a successful practitioner of everything I discuss in this book—not consistently. I have implemented much of the lifestyle I recommend here in my day-to-day life, but some aspects are still more aspirational in nature. But Paul was not perfect, either, when he told believers in 1 CORINTHIANS 11:1, "Be imitators of me, just as I also am of Christ." I believe that God wants me to help others by recording the principles that have guided me.

For many years I had this quotation from Theodore Roosevelt on my desk:

> It is not the critic who counts; not the man who points out how the strong man stumbles, or where the doer of deeds could have done them better. The credit belongs to the man who is actually in the arena, whose face is marred by dust and sweat and blood; who strives valiantly; who errs, who comes short again and again, because there is no effort without error and shortcoming; but who does actually strive to do the deeds; who knows great enthusiasms, the great devotions; who spends himself

in a worthy cause; who at the best knows in the end the triumph of high achievement, and who at the worst, if he fails, at least fails while daring greatly, so that his place shall never be with those cold and timid souls who neither know victory nor defeat.

In that sense, I am a practitioner. I try. Over the years, I have seen progress in my personal walk with God. That gives me great hope and anticipation. My prayer is that in reading what follows you will not become discouraged by gaps between the challenges I describe and your current state of progress, but rather that you will be drawn into a glorious pursuit of the amazing opportunity before us to know and love and serve God more passionately every day.

Although this book is aspirational, it is not merely descriptive. It is prescriptive. I firmly believe the matters I discuss in this book are meant to be pursued and practiced by every follower of Christ, for His pleasure.

ACKNOWLEDGMENTS

Of course, every person I mention here is a gift and creation of the Lord. Ultimately all the gratitude and honor is due to Him. He is the source of every good thing.

My wife, Debie, is the biggest earthly influence on me and my best friend. She is my complement in so many ways and a support and encouragement in a variety of ways—both obvious and unnoticed, visible and invisible.

My parents modeled lives that showed they were serious about stewarding their lives for the Lord. That was a great foundation.

My children and grandchildren (present and future) are another major influence in my life. Much of what I have learned about being a child of God has been shaped by my own experience of being a father and grandfather.

My editors, Bruce Barron and Mark Aspinwall, provided very practical assistance in helping me structure and communicate the message of this book more effectively than I ever could have done alone. Bruce took the first swing at it, and his kind but firm guidance was much needed. Mark provided invaluable input too, as I tried to figure out how to prioritize input from others and make the application sections more usable. It was also extremely helpful that he is an accomplished practitioner of the approaches covered in the book. He made it more readable as well.

I appreciate the Kingdom heart and loving service provided by the folks at William Carey Publishing, including Denise Wynn, Melissa Hicks, Andrew Sloan, Katie McGaffey, and Mike Riester.

I am grateful for the many hundreds of partners in Kingdom advance whom I have trained, mentored, and co-labored with. These men and women, who invest their lives in making disciples and planting churches in literally every nation and territory on earth, have been my friends and encouragers and have continually spurred me on to greater love and good works. Collectively they have been used to catalyze about one thousand movements, resulting in over five million house churches planted and over eighty million people baptized over the past thirty years. It has been an honor and privilege to know and work with them.

I will call out one name, the late—Steve Smith—to represent this entire group, because he typifies them. We were about the same age. I got to know Steve as I was training him at a one-month Strategy Coordinator training event in Asia back in the 1990s. I then mentored him for a while, but he quickly became a coworker and an accomplished practitioner, trainer, leader, and author. (His last book, *Spirit Walk*, written in 2018, addresses similar issues to this book.) Our families vacationed together. We worked in the same country for several years. We cheered one another on from a distance.

More recently, as Steve launched the 24:14 coalition to help coalesce many of the movements that had emerged from common roots in the early 1990s, we began spending more time together again when he asked me to serve as a co-facilitator. As soon as it was launched his cancer was discovered, and less than eighteen months later he passed into glory. He will be sorely missed by many of us whom his life touched deeply. He was a hero of the Kingdom.

Finally, I am thankful for those of you who are reading this book. I am honored to be given the opportunity to speak to you through these pages. To the extent that you apply the lessons contained in this book and pass them on to others, it will bless me; and for that I am grateful.

Curtis Sergeant
March 13, 2019

HOW TO READ THIS BOOK

This book is about putting the Christian life into daily action. It is intended to change the daily patterns of your life. Therefore, if you read it and think about it, but do not make specific plans to change your life patterns, you will not gain the intended benefit.

After you read each chapter, I suggest that you stop and reflect on it to plan specific action steps. Your reflection time should consist of the following aspects:

1. Read the questions that follow each chapter and record your responses in a journal (either physical or electronic).
2. Spend time in prayer, asking the Lord what He wants you to learn, apply, and share from the chapter. Then listen quietly.
   a. What specific action does He want you to take? This could be as simple as memorizing a relevant Bible verse or as large as moving to Afghanistan. Avoid generalities. Ask God to show you your next specific, measurable step forward. Ask God to show you when He wants you to take that step. The goal is to move from a wish (e.g., "I should love God more") to a plan (e.g., "Tonight I will set my alarm thirty minutes earlier, so I have time to pray in the morning").
   b. Ask God for the name of at least one person with whom He wants you to share an idea from that chapter, what idea that is, and when you should share it.
   c. Note these actions and dates in your journal and on your calendar.
   d. Ask the Lord to enable you to follow through on these commitments and to prepare the hearts of those with whom you intend to share insights.
   e. (Optional) If you are going through the book with others, share with them what you have heard from the Lord and the commitments you have made. Take a few moments to pray together regarding those commitments. Decide when you and your colleagues will check on each other's progress (this may often be when you meet to discuss the next chapter).
3. Before starting a new chapter, open your journal and review the commitments from the previous chapters. If you have missed any of the original target dates, schedule new dates.

At the beginning and end of each chapter, you will be reminded to take these steps.

Note that the Contents and Implementation Chart on the Table of Contents page should be used to track your progress in processing, applying, teaching, and multiplying each chapter. This book is intended to change your life and the lives of those you relate to.

I hope you will not find this book difficult to read. It is not complicated. The challenge will be to put it into practice. The implications of giving one's whole life to Christ can be unsettling. I hope you will embrace the challenge. There is nothing better or more important that you can do with your life than to accept the challenge of Theopraxy—to give all you have, every day, to living fully for God.

AN INTRODUCTION TO THEOPRAXY

Theopraxy *is a life lived in, by, and for God—*
a life focused solely on God.

There is one body and one Spirit, just as also you were called in one hope of your calling; one Lord, one faith, one baptism, one God and Father of all who is over all and through all and in all.

—Ephesians 4:4–6

Do you struggle to balance all the commitments and responsibilities of your life? Are you constantly trying to juggle and multitask to meet life's demands? What if there was only one thing you had to do well? Would that simplicity be desirable?

Jesus apparently thought so, because He told us to live that way. He invited us to give up our focus on all other things and concentrate only on Him—on knowing Him and following Him. That is what this book is about.

Theopraxy (literally, "God-practice") is a lifestyle that seeks to know Christ, to imitate Him, to seek God's Kingdom, and to view everything in life from God's perspective. It requires a desire to live in total concord with and submission to His will, ways, purposes, character, nature, desires, and thoughts. It is doing God's work, in God's way, in God's timing, by God's enablement.

The Theopraxic life is not easy. But it is simple. It requires learning to recognize God's voice, then doing what He says. He will ask of you only what He will enable you to do. Our biggest challenge is not that we can't do what God asks of us, but that we fail to weed out of our lives things He is not asking us to do. That is why we feel so busy and frazzled—we are doing too many things that we shouldn't do. Not that these things are bad. Often they are good—or, at worst, neutral. But they are not what God is calling us to do right now.

Theopraxy is not a common word. On the other hand, many are familiar with the term *orthopraxy*, or right practice. Orthopraxy is often contrasted with orthodoxy, or right belief. The point is that correct beliefs about God (orthodoxy) are useless if they are not paired with the actual life application of those beliefs (orthopraxy).

Theopraxy goes a step further. It addresses the motive behind the practice and the source of the ability to live out that practice. The motive is to follow God, and He is the source of the power to do so.

Jesus says,

> Not everyone who says to Me, "Lord, Lord," will enter the kingdom of heaven, but he who does the will of My Father who is in heaven will enter. Many will say to Me on that day, "Lord, Lord, did we not prophesy in Your name, and in Your name cast out demons, and in Your name perform many miracles?" And then I will declare to them, "I never knew you; depart from Me, you who practice lawlessness."
>
> —MATTHEW 7:21–23

In this passage, those being sent into eternal punishment had seemed to be doing good things and were doing them in Jesus' name. They did not do the Father's will, however. They did not listen for, and respond to, what He was asking them to do. Instead, they did what they thought He would want to be done. They did not hear because they did not listen. They did not recognize His voice because they did not know Him. In short, even if they were doing good things, they were not doing the things God asked of them. Thus, they had the wrong motive or reason for their actions. Also, they were evidently not acting through the empowerment of the Holy Spirit, but in their own strength. Thus, this passage suggests that even orthopraxy can fall short.

Theopraxy is not the heretical pseudo-religion that believes good works are God. It does not ask us to work for and earn our own salvation. It does not deny that our entrance into God's Kingdom is based solely on undeserved grace. Rather, it recognizes that repentance involves turning from devotion to or reliance on anything other than God to worshiping and depending on Him alone.

When we are devoted to and relying on God alone, our love, gratitude, and devotion is expressed in our commitment to following, serving, and pleasing Him. Our desire is to know Him more deeply and accompany Him more closely. These things can be done only through the equipping and empowerment of the Holy Spirit. This journey is Theopraxy.

My friend Gary Liederbach expresses this sentiment well in this prayer (all Scripture quotations are from NRSV):

> By Your Spirit at work within me in the mind and will and emotions of my soul, You're changing me from the inside out to have "the mind of Christ" (1 CORINTHIANS 2:16), to "bear the name of Christ" (MARK 9:41), to be filled with "the Spirit of Christ" (ROMANS 8:9), "sharing in the blood of Christ" (1 CORINTHIANS 10:16), "sharing in the body of Christ" (1 CORINTHIANS 10:16), releasing the "aroma of Christ" (2 CORINTHIANS 2:15), urged on by "the love of Christ" (2 CORINTHIANS 5:14), steadfast in "the truth of Christ" (2 CORINTHIANS 11:10), living each day in "the

grace of Christ" (GALATIANS 1:6), sharing "the gospel of Christ" (PHILIPPIANS 1:27), joining my fellow workers and servants as "partners of Christ" (HEBREWS 3:14), seeking to be "a faithful minister of Christ" (COLOSSIANS 1:7), letting the "peace of Christ" dwell in my heart (COLOSSIANS 3:15) and the "word of Christ" dwell in my spirit (COLOSSIANS 3:16), empowering me to be "crucified with Christ" (GALATIANS 2:19) so I can live my "life in Christ" more and more each day (1 CORINTHIANS 1:30). As You are, so I am to be in my world (1 JOHN 4:17). I was created for this and called to this—to be "conformed to the image" of Jesus Christ (ROMANS 8:29). Everything I do, everything I encounter, everything I overcome, and everything I become is for this purpose—for You to make me more like You each day. Every choice or challenge throughout every moment of my day is an opportunity for me to grow "to maturity, to the measure of the full stature of Christ" as I "grow up in every way into him who is the head, into Christ" (EPHESIANS 4:11–16). I can't do this, but "the one who calls [me] is faithful, and he will do this" (1 THESSALONIANS 5:24).

In Jesus' name I pray. Amen.

PART 1

INDIVIDUAL ASPECTS OF THEOPRAXY

1 An All-Encompassing Way of Life

Theopraxy is a frame of reference that defines every part of life—both what we do and why we do it.

He died for all, so that they who live might no longer live for themselves, but for Him who died and rose again on their behalf.

—2 CORINTHIANS 5:15

For the grace of God has appeared, bringing salvation to all men, instructing us to deny ungodliness and worldly desires and to live sensibly, righteously and godly in the present age, looking for the blessed hope and the appearing of the glory of our great God and Savior, Christ Jesus, who gave Himself for us to redeem us from every lawless deed, and to purify for Himself a people for His own possession, zealous for good deeds.

—TITUS 2:11–14

Jesus died to change *why* we live (2 CORINTHIANS 5:15). He died so that we would live for Him, not ourselves. And His grace is meant to change *how* we live (TITUS 2:11–14). We are to be His people, "zealous for good deeds." This is the life of Theopraxy. The Bible describes it in various ways:

- being filled with the Spirit (ACTS 2:4; 4:8, 31; 9:17; 13:9, 52);
- walking in the light (JOHN 8:12; 11:9; 12:35; EPHESIANS 5:8; 1 JOHN 1:5–7);
- walking in newness of life (ROMANS 6:4);
- walking in the Spirit (ROMANS 8:4; GALATIANS 5:16, 25);
- walking in love (ROMANS 14:15; EPHESIANS 5:2);
- walking by faith (2 CORINTHIANS 5:7);

- walking in truth (3 JOHN 1:1, 3–4);
- abiding in Christ (JOHN 15:4–7, 9–10; 1 JOHN 2:27–28; 3:6, 24; 4:13);
- abiding in the Holy Spirit (JOHN 14:17);
- abiding in the light (1 JOHN 2:10);
- abiding in the Son and the Father (1 JOHN 2:24);
- walking as Jesus walked (1 JOHN 2:6);
- walking worthy of the Lord (COLOSSIANS 1:10); and
- walking worthy of your calling (EPHESIANS 4:1).

These descriptions demonstrate that believers are to be "all in" with every aspect of their lives. Belonging to God is a comprehensive experience that controls every aspect of life.

The Theopraxic life is not an attempt to earn salvation. It is the grateful response to a loving and worthy God for His amazing grace and great mercy. Any other response would be inconceivable when we recognize what we deserve and what God gives. When people willingly live insipid lives after seemingly being redeemed by the Lord, there is reason to question the authenticity of their salvation.

As Dallas Willard said (http://www.dwillard.org/articles/individual/live-life-to-the-full), Grace is not opposed to effort. It is opposed to earning. Effort is action. Earning is attitude. The New Testament expects God's children to take action to live out their faith.

HEBREWS 6 demonstrates this point. The author speaks of the elementary aspects of faith, such as repentance and eternal life (6:1–3), but he encourages his readers to press on to maturity, which will be made visible in how they live their lives (4–9). Then, in verses 10–12, he says, "For God is not unjust so as to forget your work and the love which you have shown toward His name, in having ministered and in still ministering to the saints. And we desire that each one of you show the same diligence so as to realize the full assurance of hope until the end, so that you will not be sluggish, but imitators of those who through faith and patience inherit the promises."

God cares about our works. In fact, we are to demonstrate diligence in them. We are not to be lazy. Our diligence in doing God's works demonstrates our faith and shows that we are among those who will inherit God's promises. HEBREWS 9:14 tells us that "the blood of Christ" cleanses us "to serve the living God."

There are two grave errors that we can make here. The first is to believe that we must somehow earn our salvation. No! Salvation comes "by grace . . . through faith . . . not as a result of works" (EPHESIANS 2:8–9). The second is to think that since we are saved by grace, works don't matter— we have been saved and can now take it easy.

In our day, this second error is the more pervasive one. God calls us not to passivity, but to action—to join Him in the work of the Kingdom, now and for all eternity. Our salvation and righteousness before God depend on Christ's work, but now we are called to join Him in completing the work He has begun (COLOSSIANS 1:24).

JAMES 2:14–26 says faith without works is "dead." James is not saying that good works produce salvation, but that works demonstrate salvation. Works are a symptom of saving faith, not a source of salvation. Faith, without the accompanying actions that demonstrate faith, is an impossibility—a self-contradiction. What we believe and value and desire will have practical impact on our lives, our words, and our actions. How we allocate our time, energy, and resources reveals our true values and priorities. Our decisions demonstrate our allegiance.

In JOHN 15:1–17, Jesus tells us that we can do nothing apart from Him. This does not mean we are not to work. It means we are not to work apart from Him. In this passage, Jesus speaks as much about bearing fruit as He does about abiding. If we abide in Him, we will bear much fruit and thereby glorify Him. He repeatedly speaks of actions we are to take: lay down our lives, obey His commands, share His work, and bear fruit. Our life can find meaning only in Him and through Him. We are His, and He plans to put us to work.

The work we do for our King and the Kingdom does not earn us bragging rights. It is simply the natural result of our following Him. Jesus clearly communicated this attitude in LUKE 17:7–10:

> Which of you, having a slave plowing or tending sheep, will say to him when he has come in from the field, "Come immediately and sit down to eat"? But will he not say to him, "Prepare something for me to eat, and properly clothe yourself and serve me while I eat and drink; and afterward you may eat and drink"? He does not thank the slave because he did the things which were commanded, does he? **So you too, when you do all the things which are commanded you, say, "We are unworthy slaves; we have done** *only* **that which we ought to have done."**

Ephesians 2:8–10 illustrates the close connection between being saved by grace and being saved to join God in His work. We are not saved to sit, but to do good works which He has specifically prepared for each of us:

> For by grace you have been saved through faith; and that not of yourselves, it is the gift of God; not as a result of works, so that no one may boast. For we are His workmanship, created in Christ Jesus for good works, which God prepared beforehand so that we would walk in them.

Similarly, people often emphasize that God's love for us is unrelated to our behavior or our attitude. It is frequently expressed that God cannot love us any more or any less than He does. Although this is true of His *agape* (the primary biblical term for God-like love) loving, it is not true of His *philos* (brotherly or warm affection love) love.

God's *agape* love is independent of our worthiness. God loves all people in this way. This is clear from such passages as Matthew 5:44-45, John 3:16, and Romans 5:8. God's *philos* love for us, however, is dependent upon our response to Him. This is clear from John 16:27:

> The Father Himself loves you, because you have loved Me and have believed that I came forth from the Father.

The word *philos* is used in John 20:2 to describe Jesus' affection for John when John is referred to as the "disciple whom Jesus loved." This distinguishing characteristic set John apart. I want to have that sort of relationship with the Lord. I want to be a person He enjoys being with. I want to be pleasing to Him. Therefore I want to excel at doing what He asks. I want to be responsive to His desires. I want to be attentive to His will for me. I want to experience what Paul prayed for the Colossians in Colossians 1:9b-12a:

> That you may be filled with the knowledge of His will in all spiritual wisdom and understanding, so that you will walk in a manner worthy of the Lord, to please *Him* in all respects, bearing fruit in every good work and increasing in the knowledge of God; strengthened with all power, according to His glorious might, for the attaining of all steadfastness and patience; joyously giving thanks to the Father.

PRAYER

Lord, You died so that I would live for You. Your grace is designed to help me work with You and for Your Kingdom. Help me to remember this. Help me to live like this. I know that the life lived for You is the best possible life. But I'm often lazy or distracted or selfish. Forgive me. Show me my first steps to live a Kingdom-focused life. Give me the courage to take those steps. Then show me the next steps, and the next and the next. And give me the courage for those, as well.

QUESTIONS

Read the following questions, then pray and ask God what He wants you to learn and do. Listen quietly.

Note any commitments from the questions below in your journal. Note the dates by which you plan to fulfill those commitments.

1. Am I living for Jesus or for myself? How?

2. Am I passively waiting for my eternal reward or actively pursuing the advancement of God's Kingdom? How?

3. Do what I do and how I spend my time show that God's Kingdom is the motivating force in my life? How?

4. What specific actions does God want me to take in response to this chapter? (Note them in your journal and schedule them in your calendar.)

5. With whom (at least one name) does God want me to share what I have learned?

Ask the Lord to enable you to follow through on these commitments and to prepare the hearts of those with whom you intend to share insights.

2 We Have Only One Life to Live

Time is a precious gift to us, and it is constantly slipping away.
So it is all-important that we invest our time well.

So teach us to number our days, that we may present to You a heart of wisdom.

—Psalm 90:12

In this life, time is all we have to spend. Theopraxy demands that we spend it for God.

Only one life, 'twill soon be past.
Only what's done for Christ will last.

—refrain from "Only One Life," by C. T. Studd

This is a photograph of the statue of St. Jerome at the Church of the Nativity in Bethlehem. Jerome was the translator of the Latin Vulgate, which served as the official Catholic Scriptures for more than 1,500 years and is widely considered to be the most important translation of the entire Bible in history.

The Church of the Nativity was constructed on top of a series of tunnels and caves where Jerome had lived and worked on the translation for over thirty years. The statue of Jerome shows a human skull chained to his left ankle. According to tradition, Jerome chained the skull to his leg to

constantly remind himself of the brevity of life. His life verse was PSALM
90:12: "So teach us to number our days, that we may present to You a
heart of wisdom." His focus enabled him to make a massive impact on the
world for the Kingdom of God.

In our day, it is perhaps more difficult than ever to maintain such focus.
From New Delhi to Beijing, from Lagos to São Paulo, from London to
New York, increasing urbanization and the integration of new technology
into people's lives have led to a new sense of busyness and poverty—the
poverty of time. As I seek to disciple others and equip them to make
disciples, over and over I hear objections related to the lack of time.

Why? Every day still has twenty-four hours. Longer life expectancies and
the development of many time-saving technologies should yield a sense of
having more time rather than less. What has changed?

Jesus modeled a focused life. He repeatedly said only what He heard
from the Father and did only what He saw the Father doing (JOHN 5:19;
8:28; 12:49–50; 14:10). In living this way, He fulfilled the prophecy in
Isaiah 11 about the righteous reign of the Branch: "He will delight in the
fear of the Lord, and He will not judge by what His eyes see, nor make
a decision by what His ears hear" (ISAIAH 11:3). He lived a life based on
God's will rather than visible circumstances. We might be tempted to
think that this sort of living is inaccessible to us, but Jesus said in JOHN
16:13–14 that the Holy Spirit would enable His followers to experience
this same mode of existence.

Let's look more closely. Jesus said, "I do nothing on My own initiative,
but I speak these things as the Father taught Me" (JOHN 8:28B). "For I
did not speak on My own initiative, but the Father Himself who sent
Me has given Me a commandment as to what to say and what to speak"
(JOHN 12:49). Jesus indicated that He not only said and did everything
the Father told Him, but also that He didn't do or say anything else.
In JOHN 17:4, Jesus made this astonishing statement: "I glorified You on
the earth, having accomplished the work which You have given Me to
do." Jesus knew what the Father wanted Him to do; and He did it—and
nothing more.

In the Theopraxic life, there is no room for anything outside of what the
Lord is guiding us to. Everything we do or say or fail to do or say is either
under God's direction or outside His design for us. In EPHESIANS 2:10,
Paul speaks of the good works that God has prepared for each of us to

walk in. Since we have limited time, energy, and resources, every moment I spend outside of the works God has prepared for me to do is taking time away from what He intended for me.

We feel too busy because there simply is not enough time to do "both/ and"—that is, both what the Lord has planned for us and what we want to do. If we feel we are too busy, this may indicate that instead of limiting ourselves to what God intends, we are also seeking to do some activities that we want to do, outside the Lord's leading. As a result, we don't have enough time to do both. Similarly, if we say what we want to say rather than restricting ourselves to saying what the Lord is saying, we add to the noise around us but fail to achieve the purposes that God intends for us.

For some, these extraneous activities are bad things, sinful things. For others, they are neutral, but outside of God's leading. A common example is screen time: television, Web surfing, YouTube, Facebook, or computer games. For still others, the extraneous activities are good and noble distractions, like volunteering for a good cause or exercising. It becomes a distraction, however, if it isn't something the Lord has asked you to do but something you have chosen because you wanted to do it.

There simply isn't enough time to do what the Lord has planned for us as well as what we want to do. If we do what the Lord desires in addition to what we desire, there definitely won't be enough time, energy, or resources. This is a matter of stewardship. We need to be more in tune with the Spirit in order to fully utilize the twenty-four hours we are given each day. We need to be constantly attentive to the Lord's intentions and desires to achieve His purposes in our activities and in our communications with others.

Paul wrote,

> According to the grace of God which was given to me, like a wise master builder I laid a foundation, and another is building on it. But each man must be careful how he builds on it. For no man can lay a foundation other than the one which is laid, which is Jesus Christ. Now if any man builds on the foundation with gold, silver, precious stones, wood, hay, straw, each man's work will become evident; for the day will show it because it is to be revealed with fire, and the fire itself will test the quality of each man's work. If any man's work which he has built on it remains, he will receive a reward. If any man's work is burned up, he will suffer loss; but he himself will be saved, yet so as through fire.
>
> —1 CORINTHIANS 3:10–15

There will be eternal consequences for how we invest our time. Our daily patterns of speech and actions compose a body of work that God will evaluate on the day of judgment. It will not impact our salvation, which is secure, but it will determine our level of reward. Thus, being in tune with the Holy Spirit is important both for this life and for eternity.

Although we are never "off duty" in terms of not being on call for the Lord's work, the Creator has designed us to need rest and recreation. He knows what we need better than we do. He will frequently direct us to these activities—or to lack of activity. He made us to enjoy Him and His creation. Even in the Old Testament law, God ensured times of rest and celebration through the Sabbaths and various feasts. Our Father is loving. He delights in seeing us enjoy life.

What if we don't have confidence that we are hearing from the Lord about the use of our time? Then we simply use our best judgment. He understands where we are in terms of our ability to hear Him. As long as we are seeking to hear from Him in order to follow, He won't fault us for our uncertainty. The simple awareness that He cares about how we invest our time is helpful for us to continue to grow in maturity.

PRAYER

Father in heaven, I need Your help. I belong to You. All my time belongs to You. Yet often I spend it doing things I want, not as You lead. As a result, I feel harried and swamped. I'm confused. I have far more demands on my time than I can fulfill. But not all of those demands are from You. Teach me to hear Your voice and to recognize Your leading. Teach me to say no to the activities that are not from You and yes to those that are. Teach me to shut my mouth, except when You give me something to say. Enable me to say, like Jesus, "I only say what I hear from the Father and I only do what I see the Father doing."

QUESTIONS

Read the following questions, and then pray and ask God what He wants you to learn and do. Listen quietly.

Review your journal. Are there any past commitments you have not completed? If needed, schedule revised completion dates.

1. Do I steward my time well?

   a. Am I occupying my time with sinful activities or thoughts?

   b. Am I wasting time with neutral things?

   c. Am I spending time on good things that God has not called me to do?

   d. Is God calling me to do something that I am not doing?

2. What are the biggest areas I need to improve on in this regard? Am I saying more than I should or not saying enough? Doing more than I should or not doing enough?

3. What specific actions does God want me to take in response to this chapter? (Note them in your journal and schedule them in your calendar.)

4. With whom (at least one name) does God want me to share what I have learned?

Ask the Lord to enable you to follow through on these commitments and to prepare the hearts of those with whom you intend to share insights.

3 Knowing God Is Our Primary Pursuit

The primary pursuit of my life should be to know God—
to know Him more fully and more intimately.

Whatever things were gain to me, those things I have counted as loss for the sake of Christ. More than that, I count all things to be loss in view of the surpassing value of knowing Christ Jesus my Lord, for whom I have suffered the loss of all things, and count them but rubbish so that I may gain Christ, and may be found in Him, not having a righteousness of my own derived from the Law, but that which is through faith in Christ, the righteousness which comes from God on the basis of faith, that I may know Him and the power of His resurrection and the fellowship of His sufferings, being conformed to His death; in order that I may attain to the resurrection from the dead.

—PHILIPPIANS 3:7–11

In PHILIPPIANS 3, Paul explains that his life focused on one thing. He struggled and sacrificed and suffered to know Jesus and be "found in Him." First, Paul recites his impeccable pedigree and hard-won religious accomplishments (3:4–6); then he dismisses them as "rubbish" (literally, excrement) compared to the "surpassing value of knowing Christ Jesus." Our joy, pride, and fulfillment must not come from our talents, accomplishments, or heritage (3:1–6). Knowing Christ, and being found in Him, is the one thing—the only thing—worth living or dying for. Christ is the source of righteousness and eternal life. The path to those blessings, Paul writes, is found in knowing Him and being identified fully with Him (3:7–11). Paul recognizes that he had not yet reached his destination; but it was the one thing that occupied his every thought and his every breath.

All who follow Jesus should think this way. Paul encourages those who are "perfect," or mature, to "have this attitude" (3:15). "Brethren, join in following my example" (3:17). Paul strives toward that goal and calls all of us to pursue a deeper relationship with Christ. God does not save us to sit and relax, but to labor toward Him and with Him.

In contrast, those who live for earthly pleasures and take pride in things other than Jesus are called enemies of the cross of Christ. They are citizens of the world, not of the Kingdom of God. In the end, they will be destroyed, whereas Kingdom citizens will be transformed into the likeness of our glorious King and will be with Him forever (3:18–21).

Paul offers no middle ground. We will either live for God or for something else. Yet in the church today, many are trying to inhabit the nonexistent middle ground. This is deeply disturbing. Like the lukewarm church in Laodicea, we need to be zealous and repent (REVELATION 3:14–19). We need to listen to Jesus' voice and regain fellowship with Him (REVELATION 3:20).

The principal aim of life is to know God and respond to that knowledge. If we know Him intimately, if we understand who He is, and if we immerse ourselves in His will, ways, purposes, character, nature, desires, and thoughts—then our own will, ways, purposes, character, nature, desires, and thoughts will be shaped by His. We will become more and more like Him. To the extent that we know Him, we will be remade in His image.

We begin this process here, on earth, in part to prepare for an eternity of fellowship and worship. The degree to which we know the Lord is the degree to which He can transform us into His image. This will not happen fully until we enter eternity and awake in His presence (1 JOHN 3:2–3), but we should be beginning to experience this transformation now (ROMANS 12:2).

While we are on earth, the Lord also plans to use us to speak to others about Him. Knowing Him (Philippians 3:8) and making Him known (ACTS 20:24) is the life of a disciple. These two are connected. The better we know Him, the better we can make Him known. The more clearly we hear Him, the more clearly we can speak His words and will.

On our own, we could not possibly perceive the Lord. Only by His kindness can we receive His communication (MATTHEW 11:27). But He is eager to make Himself known. He is constantly communicating. He communicates in large, loud ways: through nature, through creation, through the rise and fall of empires, through the unfolding of human history. He also communicates quietly and intimately: through silent impressions, thoughts, and dreams; through the small gestures or facial expressions of a friend. He communicates through Scripture, through prayer, through words of fellow believers, through pain or grief.

Jesus is the final word, the fullest expression of the Father (COLOSSIANS 1:15–20). He is called the Word in JOHN 1:1 and JOHN 1:14. The author of Hebrews tells us that the Lord communicates in many ways, the greatest of which is through Christ (HEBREWS 1:1–4).

Of course, we can know God only in part. He is infinite; we are finite. As a result, we each have a mental box that limits our concept of God. The challenge is to expand that box—to better apprehend our infinite God.

The top of the box describes our view of God's ability to do big things. It needs to be raised. This is what happened to Jairus (MARK 5:22–24, 35–43; LUKE 8:41–42, 49–56) when his daughter died. Jesus told him not to be afraid and proceeded to raise her from the dead. The top of Jairus's box was raised that day.

The sides of the box describe our perception of the breadth of God's concern. The sides of our box need to be expanded. This happened to Peter in Acts 10 when, through a vision and then his encounter with Cornelius, he learned that the gospel was for Gentiles too.

The bottom of the box describes our understanding that God is concerned even about small things. The bottom of our box needs to be lowered. Our God knows how many hairs are on each person's head (MATTHEW 10:30). Nothing in all creation, no matter how small, is outside of God's concern and control. Are there areas of your life you feel are too small for God's concern?

To know God, knowledge of His Word is absolutely necessary, but not sufficient. How we respond to His Word also matters. Satan knows more

Scripture than any human, but he responded with pride and rebellion rather than grateful submission. As a result, he exists alienated from his creator. Belief is not enough either; the demons believe in God— and shudder (JAMES 2:19). Knowledge puffs up, but love builds up (1 CORINTHIANS 8:1 NRSV). To avoid this, we must cultivate the habit of responding, with humble obedience, to all that we learn.

From a biblical perspective, hearing God and obeying Him are inseparable. In fact, the Greek word for the verb "to obey" is simply an intensive form of the verb "to hear." Therefore, listening to God and responding with obedience are not optional for a follower of Christ; they are essential. Jesus said His followers would hear His voice and follow Him (JOHN 10:27). Conversely, He told a group of Jews that they did not hear God's voice because they did not belong to God (JOHN 8:47). He told His disciples that they were not merely slaves, but friends in whom He confided (JOHN 15:15). Paul says that those who are being led by the Spirit of God are sons of God (ROMANS 8:14). Peter says that believers are chosen by the sanctifying work of the Spirit to obey Jesus Christ (1 PETER 1:1–2). John says that obedience to Christ is the evidence that we truly belong to Him (1 JOHN 2:3–6).

God communicates both through His Word (the Bible) and by direct communication from the Holy Spirit. In Scripture, especially in the epistles, many times the Word and the Spirit are used interchangeably (e.g., EPHESIANS 5:18B–19 with parallel COLOSSIANS 3:16). They are not in conflict, but congruous (JOHN 3:34; EPHESIANS 6:17). Yet large segments of the church tend to emphasize one or the other: *either* knowing God through His Word (i.e., the Bible) *or* direct communication from the Holy Spirit.

Of course, saturating oneself in the Word is of tremendous importance. Without Scripture, we would be adrift in a sea of subjectivity. The Bible is an amazing gift that teaches us who God is and how He works. If we fail to prioritize knowing God through the Bible, we are shortsighted indeed.

However, since the Lord has specific intentions for each of us (EPHESIANS 2:10), we also need the moment-by-moment guidance of the Holy Spirit to apprehend His desires for us specifically. The principles and examples in the Bible are not designed to provide this type of guidance. Scripture provides the first test in discerning the voice of the Spirit, but it serves as the beginning, rather than the end, of God's conversation with us.

For example, in LUKE 4:23–27 Jesus referred to Elijah's ministry to the widow of Zarephath and to Elisha's ministry to Naaman the Syrian, saying these prophets were guided by God to those specific individuals and not to others who were far more visible and accessible. Jesus said the same thing was true of Himself. How did He know whom to heal? He heard from the Father.

The Holy Spirit speaks to different people in different ways, and to the same person in different ways at different times. For example, occasionally I wake up with a strong sense that the Lord is speaking to me through the dream I just had. On a few occasions I have made massively life-changing decisions based on dreams. However, that is a tiny fraction of what I hear from the Lord. Far more often, I hear from God through Scripture (frequently in combination with the Spirit speaking through my thoughts about particular applications), or I observe patterns in Scripture that echo what I am seeing God do around me. Or I am touched by the words of a song or a saint, or by careful consideration of something observable in the world that the Spirit highlights to me.

Because the Holy Spirit dwells within us, most often His voice is perceived simply as our own thoughts. It is, therefore, crucial to learn to recognize which thoughts are actually Him speaking to us. Hopefully, over time we will perceive God speaking in an increasing portion of our thoughts until our thought life becomes an unending conversation with the Lord. The more progress we make in this arena, the more in tune we can be with God's specific designs for our lives. If God is concerned with the number of hairs on our heads (MATTHEW 10:30; LUKE 12:7), then He likely has an opinion about my smallest daily decisions.

In addition to consistency with Scripture, the most valuable test I use for evaluating the source of my thoughts is whether they are characteristic of the fruit of the Spirit or the fruit of the flesh (GALATIANS 5:19–23). If they involve hatred, selfish ambition, sexual immorality, or other characteristics of the flesh, I can be sure these thoughts are not coming from God. Similarly, the tone of my thoughts tells me a lot. For example, the Holy Spirit convicts whereas the enemy condemns.

The best way to grow in our ability to hear God is to act on what we hear Him saying. He knows our limitations and our weaknesses. He will not ask something huge from us if we are unsure of His voice. He is patient. If we fail to do what He tells us, however, we will remain stunted in our ability to hear and follow Him. On the other hand, if we act on what we hear from Him, He will speak more clearly to us in the future and begin to ask more of us. This is the path to intimacy with the Lord. Developing sensitivity to God's voice is a journey that we will not complete until we see Him face-to-face. We are "on the way" or "in process" until then.

All around us, God is constantly acting and working to make Himself known and glorified. Therefore, we are continually surrounded by opportunities to perceive Him and understand Him more fully. To what extent are we discerning God's activity around us and in the world? What are we learning about Him? How is what we learn about God impacting what we do, think, say, and are becoming?

If we want to know and obey God, then we are His disciples, His followers. But how can we possibly follow someone if we cannot see or hear him? Happily, God is incessantly at work all around us at every level, from the cosmological to the subatomic. He is perpetually speaking; we just need ears to hear.

To the degree that we discern His expressions, we can respond meaningfully. Our faithfulness in doing so is the life of a disciple. It is literally a life full of faith. It is a life based not on the temporal things our eyes can see around us, but on the unseen, eternal realities He reveals to us.

PRAYER

Father in heaven, You have put Your Spirit in our hearts, crying out toward You, "Abba," "Daddy." Yet though our souls long for You, we are so often drawn away by the things around us. I am ashamed to admit that I spend most of my time, energy, and effort pursuing other things besides You. Forgive me. Change me. Please change my heart and cause me to seek You wholly, with all that I have. Wrench out of my life the things that keep me from You, even though I cling to them tightly and love them dearly. For deep down I know that only You have what I need. Teach me to recognize Your voice and obey. And as I obey, teach me to know You and hear You more clearly.

QUESTIONS

Read the following questions, then pray and ask God what He wants you to learn and do. Listen quietly.

Review your journal. Are there any past commitments you have not completed? If needed, schedule revised completion dates.

1. Is knowing Jesus the most important thing in my life?

2. How often and how clearly do I hear and recognize God's voice in my daily living?

3. How can I listen more faithfully for His voice?

4. What specific actions does God want me to take in response to this chapter? (Note them in your journal and schedule them in your calendar.)

5. With whom (at least one name) does God want me to share what I have learned?

Ask the Lord to enable you to follow through on these commitments and to prepare the hearts of those with whom you intend to share insights.

4 God's Kingdom Is Our Compass

*God's eternal Kingdom is the guiding reality
for living in this temporal world.*

Therefore we do not lose heart, but though our outer man is
decaying, yet our inner man is being renewed day by day.
For momentary, light affliction is producing for us an eternal
weight of glory far beyond all comparison, while we look not at
the things which are seen, but at the things which are not seen;
for the things which are seen are temporal, but the things which
are not seen are eternal.

—2 Corinthians 4:16–18

The Kingdom of God is counterintuitive in many ways. In God's
Kingdom:

The way to be great is to serve (Matthew 20:25–28).

The way to be strong is to be weak (2 Corinthians 12:9–10).

The way to be rich is to give everything away (Mark 10:21).

The way to be wise is to become a fool (1 Corinthians 1:18–25).

The way to be joyful is to weep (Luke 6:20–26).

The way to be first is to be last (Mark 9:35).

The way to win is to lose (Luke 9:25).

The way to live is to die (Matthew 10:38–39).

God's own plan to save us is counterintuitive. The infinitely powerful creator of everything chose to make Himself known by taking human flesh and being born as a helpless baby into an impoverished family. Jesus grew up in obscurity, spent three years as an itinerant teacher, and was then cruelly tortured and killed. But His death turned out to be the pivot point of history. By dying, Jesus overcame death, assured His own eternal reign, and provided for our eternal salvation. That is an unexpected storyline.

To live a life of Theopraxy, we must learn to think counterintuitively. We must learn to focus on, and base our lives upon, an unseen spiritual reality. The twelve spies in NUMBERS 13 are an example. Ten reported on the facts they had seen and drew the logical conclusion: "We are not able to go up against the people, for they are too strong for us" (NUMBERS 13:31). But two of the spies, Joshua and Caleb, came to a different conclusion: "The Lord is with us; do not fear them" (NUMBERS 14:9). They saw the same facts—the same giants and great walled cities. But they viewed those facts through the lens of the invisible spiritual reality: "The Lord is with us." The ten spies' failure to view things from God's perspective caused the whole nation of Israel to wander in the wilderness for forty years until their entire generation died off.

In 2 KINGS 6, when the king of Aram sent his army to kill Elisha, Elisha's servant was worried. Elisha prayed for his servant's eyes to be opened, and he saw chariots of fire—the armies of the Lord—surrounding them for protection. Because Elisha was aware of the unseen army, he was completely unconcerned about the enemy that could be seen. This attitude led to his audacious response of praying for them to be blinded and leading them to his own king. He then proceeded to instruct the king to treat the enemy combatants as honored guests and send them home in peace. This encounter resulted in a period of respite from the war.

In MATTHEW 14:28–33, we have another example. There, Peter briefly walks on water. He sees Jesus walking over the waves. At Jesus' invitation, Peter steps out of the boat to walk on the water toward Jesus. But seeing the wind, he became frightened and began to sink. Jesus took hold of Peter and said to him, "You of little faith, why did you doubt?" Think about that. Jesus rebukes Peter for doubting that, with Jesus' help, he could walk on water. Jesus wanted Peter to know that His unseen power was greater than the visible power of wind, waves, and gravity. And He wanted Peter to act confidently on that knowledge. This is action based on an alternate reality. Living based on the Kingdom of God, rather than earthly realities, requires heavenly enablement.

The challenge in being Theopraxic is to keep our eyes fixed on Jesus and the eternal realities of the Kingdom, and to live accordingly (HEBREWS 12:1–11; 2 CORINTHIANS 4:7–18; COLOSSIANS 3:1–4). That is the life of faith (HEBREWS 11:1–3). We cannot please God in any other way (HEBREWS 11:6). Living such a life is the evidence that we believe God and are relying on, seeking, serving, loving, and worshiping Him alone.

Midway through the great "hall of faith" in Hebrews 11, the author explains what all of the great heroes of the faith have in common:

> All these died in faith, without receiving the promises, but having seen them and having welcomed them from a distance, and having confessed that they were strangers and exiles on the earth. For those who say such things make it clear that they are seeking a country of their own… . But as it is, they desire a better country, that is, a heavenly one. Therefore God is not ashamed to be called their God; for He has prepared a city for them. (HEBREWS 11:13–16)

Because these great saints were focused on the invisible future promises of God, and not the visible here and now, "God is not ashamed to be called their God."

The focus of this life of faith is exclusively on Jesus, as HEBREWS 12:1–11 explains. It requires us to "lay aside every encumbrance and the sin which so easily entangles us." We are to do away with anything that would distract or hinder us—even good things—just as Jesus did only what He saw the Father doing and said only what He heard the Father saying.

We are to focus exclusively on running the race that He has set before us. In doing so, we are to rely steadfastly on Jesus, remembering how He looked forward to the joy before Him and despised the suffering and shame He had to endure.

The author of Hebrews reminds us of the struggles we will face both in resisting sin and persisting in the face of discipline from the Father. But he promises that God's discipline comes from fatherly love, will result in our increasing holiness, and will eventually yield the "peaceful fruit of righteousness" (HEBREWS 12:11) as the Lord achieves His aim in our lives. Those are indeed reassuring incentives for submitting wholeheartedly to His pruning.

SECOND CORINTHIANS 4:7–12, 16–18 echoes the same themes. Paul does not shy away from the difficulties we are destined to experience as we live the life of faith:

But we have this treasure in earthen vessels, so that the surpassing greatness of the power will be of God and not from ourselves; we are afflicted in every way, but not crushed; perplexed, but not despairing; persecuted, but not forsaken; struck down, but not destroyed; always carrying about in the body the dying of Jesus, so that the life of Jesus also may be manifested in our body. For we who live are constantly being delivered over to death for Jesus' sake, so that the life of Jesus also may be manifested in our mortal flesh. So death works in us, but life in you... . Therefore we do not lose heart, but though our outer man is decaying, yet our inner man is being renewed day by day. For momentary, light affliction is producing for us an eternal weight of glory far beyond all comparison, while we look not at the things which are seen, but at the things which are not seen; for the things which are seen are temporal, but the things which are not seen are eternal.

Paul willingly makes the sacrifices necessary to live the life of faith because he knows the unseen things are more permanent, more secure, and more solid than the things he can see and touch and taste. He considers the shipwrecks, stonings, beatings, imprisonment, and hunger he has endured as "light" and "momentary" compared to the "eternal weight of glory" that is stored up as a result. To Paul, the unseen things are more real than the seen—and he lives his life accordingly.

In 1 CORINTHIANS 15:50–57, Paul explains how "in a moment, in the twinkling of an eye" our mortal bodies will be exchanged for immortal ones. In verse 58, he concludes, "Therefore [because of the promised eternal reward], my beloved brethren, be steadfast, immovable, always abounding in the work of the Lord, knowing that your toil is not in vain in the Lord." Our promised future is a motive for Kingdom living now.

FIRST CORINTHIANS 9:24–27 also implores us to concentrate our efforts on Kingdom matters:

Do you not know that those who run in a race all run, but only one receives the prize? Run in such a way that you may win. Everyone who competes in the games exercises self-control in all things. They then do it to receive a perishable wreath, but we an imperishable. Therefore I run in such a way, as not without aim; I box in such a way, as not beating the air; but I discipline my body and make it my slave, so that, after I have preached to others, I myself will not be disqualified.

Paul explains that this disciplined focus is driven by his desire to avoid the mistakes made by the Israelites during the Exodus (1 CORINTHIANS 10:1–12). All of them were "baptized into Moses." All of them drank "spiritual drink" and ate "spiritual food." "Nevertheless, with most of them God was not well-pleased; for they were laid low in the wilderness." Their membership in the nation of Israel, crossing the Red Sea, eating manna, drinking the water that miraculously poured out of the rock, and participation in the miracles of Moses were not enough to make them acceptable to God. God was displeased because they craved evil things, persisted in idol worship, and grumbled against God (VERSES 6, 7, 10).

We need to avoid the same mistake. *"Now these things happened to them as an example, and they were written for our instruction, upon whom the ends of the ages have come. Therefore let him who thinks he stands take heed that he does not fall"* (VERSES 11–12). We too can miss the promised land. We too can miss the blessing God has for us, if we fail to focus on Him and His Kingdom and allow ourselves to be distracted.

COLOSSIANS 3:1–4 similarly redirects our focus to the Kingdom of heaven:

> Therefore if you have been raised up with Christ, keep seeking the things above, where Christ is, seated at the right hand of God. Set your mind on the things above, not on the things that are on earth. For you have died and your life is hidden with Christ in God. When Christ, who is our life, is revealed, then you also will be revealed with Him in glory.

The recurrent theme is unmistakable: die to self while here on earth, with an eye on the eternal hope of glory with God. This is why Paul wrote that faith, hope, and love endure forever (1 CORINTHIANS 13:13). Love is the ultimate characteristic of God's Kingdom, but faith is the means of living the life He gives, and hope gives the strength to persist in that life.

As we live a life of Theopraxy, we have but one purpose: God's purpose. As Paul told Timothy, "Suffer hardship with *me*, as a good soldier of Christ Jesus. No soldier in active service entangles himself in the affairs of everyday life, so that he may please the one who enlisted him as a soldier" (2 TIMOTHY 2:3–4). This message is concerned primarily with focusing Timothy's attention. Paul is making sure Timothy will not be distracted by earthly matters and lose his focus on eternal matters.

This focus can be illustrated by the process of pruning. For a time, I worked as a berry farmer. I have some advice for you: If you are going to grow berries, do not start with blackberries. Growing them is extremely labor-intensive. You have to set up a trellis system with two wires and place a berry plant every six feet, next to a pole. Every year, the plant puts out multiple "canes." You have to prune off all but two of the canes and then train these two to climb the pole. As they grow, you tie them onto the pole while trimming any additional shoots that emerge. Then you train them along the wires, one cane to each wire. Again, you constantly trim any extraneous shoots. Over the course of a season, a blackberry farmer might trim 90 percent of the growth so as to end up with only growth along the poles and wires.

In the end, this work is rewarded with an abundant harvest along every pole and wire. Without the support system, the plant would not be able to carry so much fruit. The berries are huge and juicy. All the berries are readily accessible and can be harvested quickly and easily.

We also have wild blackberries in our part of the country. The berries are much smaller. There are only a few blackberries per plant. To pick them, you have to fight your way through the thorns and brambles. You can pick as many carefully cultivated blackberries in five minutes as you can pick wild blackberries in two hours. But to get to that point, a significant commitment is involved—not only the brutal pruning process I have already described, but after the harvest you have to cut down all of the past season's growth and start all over again. Achieving that sort of harvest requires a significant degree of discipline.

It is possible to follow Christ in a convenient, casual, and lazy fashion, sort of like growing wild blackberries. You may yield some fruit, but the result will never be comparable to that of a life wholly set apart for His purposes and pleasure.

Jesus uses a similar metaphor in JOHN 15. He says, "I am the true vine, and My Father is the vinedresser. Every branch in Me that does not bear fruit, He takes away; and every *branch* that bears fruit, He prunes it so that it may bear more fruit." In Jesus' story, we are not the farmer; we are the branches, or canes, that must be pruned to bear fruit. God the Father is the farmer who prunes for fruitfulness, and Jesus is the vine from whom all the branches grow and draw sustenance.

If our goal is fruitfulness in God's Kingdom, we must be ready for pruning. We need to willingly submit to painful discipline from our loving Father, who "*disciplines us* for *our* good, so that we may share His holiness" (HEBREWS 12:10). Sanctification (becoming holy in our daily lives) may involve changing our behavior, as in the passages that call us to "put off" our old ways and "put on" a new life (e.g., EPHESIANS 4:20–32; COLOSSIANS 3:8–17). But often it will require inner change. It may mean doing the same things, but doing them for God rather than for oneself.

Jesus warned that some people, on the day of judgment, will claim to have been doing the right things but will still be rejected by God. They will say, "Lord, Lord, did we not prophesy in Your name, and in Your name cast out demons, and in Your name perform many miracles?" And yet, Jesus will say, "I never knew you" (MATTHEW 7:22–23).

Religious activities and spiritual actions do not prove allegiance to God, nor are miraculous blessings necessarily a sign of God's pleasure. In MATTHEW 11:20–24, Jesus rails against the cities where most of His miracles occurred because they did not repent. He said those miracles would simply result in heavier judgment against those cities. *Without repentance and commitment, even God's blessings are a punishment, just as suffering for the cause of Christ is actually a reward* (MATTHEW 5:10–12; ACTS 5:41; 2 CORINTHIANS 4:17).

I understand why some people are enamored with signs and wonders, but I have never really been very interested in them. Many people wish they could have witnessed Jesus' miracles firsthand. I also wish I could have followed Him on earth, but for a very different reason. I would love to have witnessed what it looked like for someone to live a perfect life of Theopraxy. How did He demonstrate a perfect expression of the Father's will in every moment, in every interaction, in the use of His time and energy and resources? How did He do business, do carpentry, or tell a joke? What did He talk about when hanging out with people? What does it look like for a human to live in this world as a perfect citizen of the heavenly Kingdom?

Similarly, when reading a missionary newsletter, many people love photos, tolerate text, and abhor spreadsheets or statistics. I am the opposite. I rarely even look at the photos. After all, a lineup of the participants in some training session looks just like any of a hundred other similar photos I have seen. I seek out the text and devour the spreadsheets or statistics. To me, those reveal much more about what is happening than a mere photo. God has preferences as well. He sees appearances, He notices actions, but He looks primarily at the heart (1 SAMUEL 16:7).

In Theopraxy, we serve an audience of one. It is possible to do the same action either for God or for oneself or some other purpose. If we do everything for the glory of God, God sees. Then our lives become an act of worship. Our whole lives can be a prayer (1 CORINTHIANS 10:31).

Jesus described the hearts of men with the parable of the four soils (MATTHEW 13:3–23; MARK 4:3–25; LUKE 8:5–15). Failure to hear or receive the word reveals a hard heart. Hard times and deprivation reveal shallow hearts. Easy times and prosperity reveal distracted hearts. Only through the Holy Spirit can we have good hearts that produce the fruitful crop the Lord desires. God invests more in those who are faithful. So how can we cultivate our hearts?

Above all, God delights in humble hearts. In MATTHEW 11, Jesus says God has revealed His works to "infants" and hidden them from "the wise and intelligent" (VERSES 25–26). He adds that no one knows either the Father or the Son unless the Son reveals them (VERSE 27). Then Jesus tells us that He calls those "who are weary and heavy-laden" (VERSE 28). Those people are like Him, for He is humble in heart. Those are the people to whom He will give rest. He will teach them and carry their loads. Again, a life totally devoted to God is ironic. It is impossible to live in one's own strength, yet living in God is easy and light (VERSES 29–30).

It has always been this way. Moses was God's friend (EXODUS 33:11) and the most humble man on earth (NUMBERS 12:3). God gave him an enormous task and helped him bear the burden (NUMBERS 11:11–14). The same pattern holds true throughout Scripture. Those who know the Lord the best are the humblest. These people are often called on to make the greatest sacrifices, but are also used in mighty ways.

Living for an audience of one means living as extremists from the world's perspective. This is an attitude of the heart. It exposes our level of commitment, our determination to pursue one goal. Jesus said, "From the days of John the Baptist until now the kingdom of heaven suffers violence, and violent men take it by force" (MATTHEW 11:12). We may not say it in quite such a jarring way, but no matter how we express it, total commitment to Christ sounds offensive to the world. Our level of commitment is exhibited by the level of sacrifice we are willing to make or the level of risk we are willing to take for His sake.

PRAYER

Father in heaven, though I cannot see You, You and Your promises are stronger and more reliable than anything I can see or touch or taste. You are the ultimate reality. Your Kingdom is the most important thing in the universe. Eternity with You is so much bigger and longer than this life. But my fears and desire for comfort push me to focus on what is right in front of me. Teach me to live a life of faith. Teach me to willingly suffer now to gain the great reward You promise me. Teach me to accept from Your hand the discipline I need to become the person You made me to be. Prepare me for life with You. Do what is necessary to wrench the roots of my heart from this temporal world and transplant them in eternity. Thank You for loving me, forgiving me, adopting me, and giving me a future with You.

QUESTIONS

Read the following questions, then pray and ask God what He wants you to learn and do. Listen quietly.

Review your journal. Are there any past commitments you have not completed? If needed, schedule revised completion dates.

1. Do I make my daily decisions based primarily on earthly or eternal realities? How do my daily activities demonstrate that?

2. What am I doing, in my life, that would be completely crazy if Jesus' promises were not true?

3. What specific actions does God want me to take in response to this chapter? (Note them in your journal and schedule them in your calendar.)

4. With whom (at least one name) does God want me to share what I have learned?

Ask the Lord to enable you to follow through on these commitments and to prepare the hearts of those with whom you intend to share insights.

5 Our Enemies Are Fear and Pride

Fear is an insult to God; pride is a challenge to God.

> "Have I not commanded you? Be strong and courageous! Do not tremble or be dismayed, for the Lord your God is with you wherever you go."
>
> —JOSHUA 1:9

> "God is opposed to the proud, but gives grace to the humble." Submit therefore to God. Resist the devil and he will flee from you. Draw near to God and he will draw near to you.
>
> —JAMES 4:6–8

Fear and pride are two key issues that hinder a Theopraxic life. Most people are heavily affected by one or the other. Personally, I am far more susceptible to pride than to fear.

Both fear and pride are really a cluster, or family, of sins. For example, in missions circles, we often refer to guilt-based cultures and shame-based cultures. Guilt is an expression of fear. Guilt fears condemnation and punishment. Shame is an expression of pride. It seeks honor and glory for itself both individually and corporately.

Fear results from not having a high enough apprehension of God's power, presence, goodness, trustworthiness, or concern. As such, it is an insult to God. The Bible is full of instances where people trusted in men, money, or human power rather than in God. This behavior is a direct outgrowth of fear, because it usually happens when we turn to men, money, or power to deliver us from what we fear.

MARK 4:35–41 illustrates Jesus' perspective on fear. He and the disciples got into a boat. Jesus was tired, so he fell asleep on a cushion in the back of the boat. As He was sleeping, a storm arose and the waves began to wash over the sides of the vessel, threatening to swamp it. Frightened, the disciples woke Jesus, demanding "Teacher, do You not care that we are perishing?" Jesus got up, rebuked the storm, and everything became calm. Then Jesus asked His disciples: "Why are you afraid? Do you still have no faith?"

Apparently, Jesus thought fear was not an appropriate response for people in a small boat amidst a big storm with waves washing over the sides. To the rest of us, this response seems completely normal, even inevitable. But why? Jesus does not say, "Why are you afraid? You are all experienced fishermen who have been in many storms bigger than this." He says, "Why are you afraid? Do you still have no faith?" Note the word *still*. Jesus seems offended that, after knowing Him and seeing Him do many miracles, the disciples still lack faith and grow afraid when a storm comes up. The antidote to fear is faith in God, not self-confidence.

We see this message throughout the Scriptures. When God called Moses to deliver Israel from Egypt, Moses was afraid. He asked, "Who am I, that I should go to Pharaoh, and that I should bring the sons of Israel out of Egypt?" (EXODUS 3:11). God answered: "Certainly I will be with you" (EXODUS 3:12). When Joshua was ordered to bring Israel into the promised land, God encouraged him, saying, "Be strong and courageous! Do not tremble or be dismayed, for the Lord your God is with you wherever you go" (JOSHUA 1:9).

Moses and Joshua had ample reason to be afraid. Egypt and the nations of Canaan were far more powerful than Israel. But they could be brave because they had faith in God who was with them. To fear is to doubt God's power or goodness.

Our conception of God and how we respond to Him define our lives. When we live in fear, we display deficiencies in our understanding of God.

If fear (or trusting in something or someone other than God) is an *insult* to God, pride is a *challenge* to God. When we exhibit pride, we put ourselves in the place of trust and honor. We put ourselves in competition with the Lord. Scripture tells us that God opposes the proud but gives grace to the humble (JAMES 4:6; 1 PETER 5:5).

In *Mere Christianity*, C. S. Lewis refers to pride as the cardinal sin and notes that it is characteristic of Satan himself. He adds that humility, the opposite of pride, does not mean thinking little of ourselves, but thinking of ourselves little. A proud person's constant point of reference is himself or herself, not God. Therefore, a proud person cannot live a life of Theopraxy.

Three times in his writings, Paul broadly compares himself with others. The first time, relatively early in his ministry, he categorizes himself as the least of the apostles (1 CORINTHIANS 15:9). Around the middle of his ministry, he classifies himself as the least of all saints (EPHESIANS 3:8). Finally, toward the end of his life, he calls himself the greatest of sinners (1 TIMOTHY 1:15).

Compared to other people, these comments are simply untrue. Paul was one of the most consecrated and fruitful missionaries in human history. From heaven's perspective, however, these comments make perfect sense. The more mature Paul became, the more he thought of himself in comparison to God and the more fully he understood what that meant. Hence his trust in and regard for himself continued to decrease as he loved, trusted, and relied on God more and more completely.

Pride puts us in a position of competing with God for glory. We cannot expect a relationship with God if we are competing with Him.

> For thus says the high and exalted One
>
> Who lives forever, whose name is Holy,
>
> "I dwell on a high and holy place,
>
> And also with the contrite and lowly of spirit ..."
>
> —ISAIAH 57:15

The eternal, high, exalted, and holy God lives in two places: the "high and holy place" and "with the contrite and lowly of spirit." If we hope to have God present with us, we must make sure that our hearts are contrite and lowly of spirit, for only then will God dwell with us.

In this passage, and many others, the Bible plainly teaches that God will make Himself known to us only if we have a high opinion of Him and a comparatively low opinion of ourselves. For example:

> The LORD is near to the brokenhearted
>
> And saves those who are crushed in spirit.
>
> —PSALM 34:18

"Blessed are the poor in spirit, for theirs is the kingdom of heaven.

Blessed are those who mourn, for they shall be comforted."

—MATTHEW 5:3–4

"But the tax collector, standing some distance away, was even unwilling to lift up his eyes to heaven, but was beating his breast, saying, 'God, be merciful to me, the sinner!' I tell you, this man went to his house justified rather than the other; for everyone who exalts himself will be humbled, but he who humbles himself will be exalted."

—LUKE 18:13–14

Developing a proper view of ourselves is a problem in this current era of self-esteem and positive thinking. We want to know God, but we also want to hang on to our high opinion of ourselves. That is not an option. God does not befriend proud people. In fact, by clinging to our pride, we make God our opponent, our enemy.

"God is opposed to the proud, but gives grace to the humble." Submit therefore to God. Resist the devil and he will flee from you. Draw near to God and He will draw near to you.

—JAMES 4:6–8

If we humble ourselves before the Lord, He will draw near to us. If we persist in thinking that we are good, God will keep His distance.

Why is God so insistent on this point? Why will He become intimate only with those who think themselves small and unworthy? God wants us to be humble not because it boosts His ego, but simply because humility befits our nature. God is perfectly good, utterly powerful, and our Creator and Savior. We are the weak and sinful creatures He has redeemed by His own death. He is not willing to humor us by entering a relationship based on the polite pretense that we are good.

From God's perspective, pride is utterly ridiculous. In ISAIAH 10:15, the Lord aptly describes the pride of the king of Assyria: "Is the axe to boast itself over the one who chops with it? Is the saw to exalt itself over the one who wields it? *That would be* like a club wielding those who lift it, *or* like a rod lifting *him who* is not wood." We have no ability, no skill, no knowledge, other than what was given to us by the Lord. Apart from Him, we can do *nothing* (JOHN 15:5).

In the end, when the truth about God is fully revealed, there will be no room for human pride. Isaiah makes this clear when he describes the coming of the Lord in the last days.

> The proud look of man will be abased,
> And the loftiness of man will be humbled,
> And the LORD alone will be exalted in that day.
> For the LORD of hosts will have a day of reckoning
> Against everyone who is proud and lofty
> And against everyone who is lifted up,
> That he may be abased.
>
> —ISAIAH 2:11–12

For now, the truth about God is invisible to those who reject Him. Thus they persist in the proud delusion that they are good and worthy. When God reveals Himself in His holiness, glory, and power, previously proud people will drop in dismay, instantly perceiving the absurdity of their conceit. Then pride will no longer be possible. Those who wish to know God now must now adopt the humility that ultimately will be imposed on everyone. To live a life of Theopraxy, we must do battle with fear and pride.

I knew a coach who frequently said, "Fatigue makes cowards of us all." He was correct. Nothing exposes my deficiencies more starkly than profound fatigue. On several occasions, God has allowed me to experience extended seasons of extreme fatigue. That experience produces a sense of inadequacy, which may be God's way of addressing my propensity to pride. When fatigued, I clearly recognize my complete and desperate need for Him, and I acknowledge His invitation to be with Him. He is constantly calling, "Come to Me, all who are weary and heavy-laden, and I will give you rest. Take My yoke upon you and learn from Me, for I am gentle and humble in heart, and you will find rest for your souls. For My yoke is easy and My burden is light" (MATTHEW 11:28–30).

Notice that Jesus says *His* purpose, *His* yoke, *His* burden, is light. He does not promise to give us strength for our own desires apart from Him. The strength He will provide, even in our weakness and fatigue, is for the purpose of doing His will.

There are many practical ways to cultivate humility and counteract pride in our daily lives. Ask for or accept assistance from others. Be grateful. Listen more. Praise others. Ask more questions. Serve others. Seek advice.

Banishing fear, on the other hand, is largely a matter of putting things into eternal perspective and comparing what we fear to God, who is bigger than all our fears.

More than anything else, being Theopraxic—constantly focused on the Lord and on His perspective—is a death knell to both fear and pride. We need to deal with these two foes forcefully and ruthlessly whenever we discover new pockets of their presence in our lives.

When I began writing this book, I spent the entire first day skimming thousands of Scripture verses related to Theopraxy. As I did so, two overarching themes came powerfully into view. The first was no surprise: Our God is the one and only God and He alone deserves all worship and honor and glory. But the second was unexpected, at least in terms of its frequency. The Bible contains hundreds of references to people who looked to the wrong source for deliverance from their desperation and fear. God wants to be recognized as the exclusive source of all good and necessary blessings, the answer to every need. He loves it when we come to Him for protection.

Here are just two examples from the Psalms. In the second, God Himself is speaking. We can hear His heart.

> God is our refuge and strength,
> A very present help in trouble.
> Therefore we will not fear, though the earth should change
> And though the mountains slip into the heart of the sea.
>
> —Psalm 46:1–2

> "Because he has loved Me, therefore I will deliver him;
> I will set him securely on high, because he has known My name.
> "He will call upon Me, and I will answer him;
> I will be with him in trouble;
> I will rescue him and honor him."
>
> —Psalm 91:14–15

Clearly, these two concepts are related, since God is both the only being worthy of worship and the source and sustainer of all creation. I also see an interesting parallel between these two issues and the sins of fear and pride. Fear correlates with seeking relief or deliverance from another source; pride corresponds with honoring another entity.

The Lord rightly desires and demands to be acknowledged as the center of the cosmos. He is the focus of every issue or concern. He is the axis of every activity. He sets the parameters for every event and interaction. Failure to recognize this most essential feature of life is a scandalous abomination, a deplorable atrocity, and a heinous violation of God's intended order.

PRAYER

Father in heaven, thank You for allowing us to call You Father. There is nothing about us that makes us deserve to be Your children. As we walk with You, You call us to be fearless (because You are with us) and humble (because You are so much greater than we are). Both are unnatural for me. Help me to focus on You, not me, and to boldly follow Your lead. It makes me a little afraid even to say it, but I depend on You. And You are dependable. Help me to clearly see the truth about myself and about You. Help me to fear only You. Help me to be humble before You, for I long to know You as only the humble can.

QUESTIONS

Read the following questions, then pray and ask God what He wants you to learn and do. Listen quietly.

Review your journal. Are there any past commitments you have not completed? If needed, schedule revised completion dates.

1. Which affects me more: fear or pride? Why?

2. What would I do differently if I were not afraid?

3. What would I do differently if I were not proud?

4. What specific actions does God want me to take in response to this chapter? (Note them in your journal and schedule them in your calendar.)

5. With whom (at least one name) does God want me to share what I have learned?

Ask the Lord to enable you to follow through on these commitments and to prepare the hearts of those with whom you intend to share insights.

6 Suffering Is Our Pathway

To live a Theopraxic life, we must fully identify with Christ,
including identification with His suffering and death.

Truly, truly, I say to you, unless a grain of wheat falls into the
earth and dies, it remains alone; but if it dies, it bears much
fruit. He who loves his life loses it, and he who hates his life in
this world will keep it to life eternal. If anyone serves Me, he
must follow Me; and where I am, there My servant will be also; if
anyone serves Me, the Father will honor him.

—JOHN 12:24–26

There are two crosses in the life of every true Christian: the cross on
which Jesus suffered and died, and the cross on which we must suffer and
die to self. Receiving Jesus is free; we need only to accept His free gift of
eternal life. To do that, however, we must repent, turn from our own way
to His way, and follow Him. And the path of following Jesus always passes
through suffering and death in this world.

The upside-down nature of the Kingdom is, by definition, a test of faith.
It requires us to live by faith rather than by sight. In PHILIPPIANS 3:10,
Paul declares that the only way we can know the Lord, be identified
with Him, and share His life is through also sharing in the "fellowship
of His sufferings" and His death. In 2 TIMOTHY 3:12, Paul gives a rarely
quoted Bible promise: "All who desire to live godly in Christ Jesus will be
persecuted."

Jesus already paid the price to cover our guilt and shame when He died on the cross. However, the pathway of a Theopraxic life has a second cross: our own. The disciples struggled to understand the two crosses. We can see their struggle in CHAPTERS 8–10 of MARK's Gospel. In his sparing, straightforward style, Mark makes the pathway plain.

MARK 8:22–26 describes an unusual, two-stage miracle. It is as if Jesus needed two attempts to heal a blind man. After the first attempt, the man can still only see vaguely; after the second try he can see clearly. I don't know all the implications of this two-stage healing miracle, but it provides an interesting analogy by which to consider the disciples' initially vague grasp of the nature of the King and His Kingdom.

In MARK 8:27–30, Jesus questions the Twelve. As if administering a midterm exam, He asks first, "Who do people say that I am?" and then "But who do you say that I am?" Peter gets a gold star for his response that "You are the Christ." So far, so good.

But surprisingly, Jesus orders the disciples not to tell anyone else that He is the Messiah. I have always been told that Jesus said this because it was not yet His time to be crucified and He therefore wanted to keep a low profile. There may be truth to that, but I think there is more to the story. Jesus prohibited the disciples from announcing that He was the Christ because, at this point in their development, they didn't understand who "the Christ" was. They would have been proclaiming a false message. They were confused about what it meant to be the Messiah and muddled about His Kingdom. It was like the blind man's vision after the first healing attempt. And Jesus didn't want them reproducing a false image of who He was.

We see the disciples' distorted understanding in MARK 8:31–33, as Jesus begins to describe His forthcoming suffering and death and resurrection. Peter, who has just recognized Jesus as the Messiah, immediately reprimands Him! That is an amazing action, one that required considerable hubris on Peter's part. In response, Jesus rebukes Peter, whom He has just praised, saying, "Get behind Me, Satan; for you are not setting your mind on God's interests, but man's" (VERSE 33).

The fact that Jesus refers to Peter as Satan shows how seriously He takes the matter. He contrasts God's interests and man's. Man's interests are in power and glory, comfort and ease. That is the path down which Peter wanted Jesus to lead them. God's interests are something different altogether—the path of suffering, death, resurrection, and glory.

Then Jesus proceeds to teach the Twelve and the crowd about the cost of following Him (MARK 8:34–38). "If anyone wishes to come after Me, he must deny himself, and take up his cross and follow Me" (VERSE 34). One cannot serve God and the things of this world too. This was the message Peter was not ready to hear or accept. This is the message of the second cross—our cross.

The Transfiguration (MARK 9:1–13) further reconfirms Jesus' identity as the Christ. Peter, always talking—especially when he doesn't know what to say—suggests that they build tents and stay on the mountain. He wants to hold on to this mountaintop experience. Jesus brings him back down to earth, reiterating that the Christ "will suffer many things and be treated with contempt" (VERSE 12) and rise from the dead (VERSE 9). The cross is again brought to the forefront.

MARK 9:14–29 describes the healing of a demon-possessed boy. The disciples ask afterwards why they had been unable to cast out the demon. Jesus replies that this can only be accomplished by prayer and fasting (see also MATTHEW 17:21), again highlighting the need for self-denial. He intends for His deliverance to come not by a triumphalistic process but through prayer, humility, and sacrifice, in complete dependence upon the Father.

Jesus then reiterates the necessity of His suffering, death, and resurrection, as if determined to help His disciples understand this central aspect of His ministry. "The Son of Man is to be delivered into the hands of men, and they will kill Him; and when He has been killed, He will rise three days later" (MARK 9:31). But the disciples were afraid and wanted Him to quit talking about death (MARK 9:32).

In MARK 9:33–37, the disciples immediately display their total lack of comprehension of Jesus' message, as they argue about which of them is the greatest. Jesus responds, "If anyone wants to be first, he shall be last of all and servant of all" (VERSE 35). In speaking to them again about humility and servanthood, He highlights that in His Kingdom serving others, not being served, is the sign of greatness. The idea of the second cross, the cross of the follower, is as abhorrent to the disciples as the first, the cross of Jesus.

Yet again the Twelve demonstrate their cluelessness as they show their proclivity for sectarianism and exclusivity in MARK 9:38–41. Jesus admonishes them and commends the grace and humility of a servant (i.e., anyone who offers them a cup of water). He then continues with

a discourse in MARK 9:42–50 that illustrates once more the path of the
cross. The only way to life, he teaches, is through denying oneself and
dying to one's own desires. The idea of the cross is clearly in view here.
Better to die than to cause a little one to stumble; better to cut off parts
of one's body than to go into eternal death. Unity and peace among those
who follow Christ are held up as evidence of their humility and thus
genuineness (VERSE 50).

MARK 10 begins with vignettes addressing marriage (10:1–12) and children
(10:13–16), which reveal a disconnect between prevailing attitudes and the
humble servanthood of a person on the path of the Kingdom.

Then, in MARK 10:17–31, we have the account of the rich young ruler who
asked Jesus, "Good Teacher, what shall I do to inherit eternal life?" They
talked back and forth, and finally, "Looking at him, Jesus felt a love for
him and said to him, 'One thing you lack: go and sell all you possess and
give to the poor, and you will have treasure in heaven; and come, follow
Me'" (VERSE 21). The young man departed sadly, because he was very rich.

Jesus loved this young man, but the young man had things backwards;
he valued riches more than Jesus. So Jesus gave him a choice. He could
keep his riches or he could sell all, follow Jesus, and gain treasure in
heaven. Jesus pointed this young man toward the second cross. But the
rich young man chose not to pick it up, and instead went away sad.
Unless we understand the two crosses, we will value the wrong things.
We live in the temporary shadows cast by lesser desires instead of in the
blazing glory of our eternal King.

In MARK 10:23, Jesus speaks of how hard it will be for the wealthy to
enter the Kingdom of God. The disciples seem rattled by Jesus' exchange
with this young man, so Jesus repeats Himself. They are confused, asking
in MARK 10:26, "Then who can be saved?" They still cannot comprehend
the two crosses.

One can sense from Peter's comment in MARK 10:28, "Behold, we have left
everything and followed You," that he feels off balance and wants to make
sure he is safe in this strange world Jesus is describing. Jesus affirms Peter's
sacrifice: "Truly I say to you, there is no one who has left house or brothers
or sisters or mother or father or children or farms, for My sake and for the
gospel's sake, but that he will receive a hundred times as much" (10:29–
30A). But then Jesus adds something Peter is not expecting: "along with
persecutions; and in the age to come, eternal life" (10:30B). Jesus concludes

by reiterating the upside-down nature of His Kingdom: "Many who are first will be last, and the last, first" (10:31). I imagine that Peter felt even more disoriented because Jesus unexpectedly included persecution in the package that comes with following the Messiah.

In MARK 10:32–34, for the fifth time since MARK 8, Jesus clearly tells the disciples about His upcoming suffering, death, and resurrection:

> And again He took the twelve aside and began to tell them what was going to happen to Him, saying, "Behold, we are going up to Jerusalem, and the Son of Man will be delivered to the chief priests and the scribes; and they will condemn Him to death and will hand Him over to the Gentiles. They will mock Him and spit on Him, and scourge Him and kill Him, and three days later He will rise again."

Immediately afterwards, James and John come to Him, asking for the best seats in the coming Kingdom. Jesus' frustration is apparent in His response: "You do not know what you are asking. Are you able to drink the cup that I drink, or to be baptized with the baptism with which I am baptized?" (MARK 10:38). But that is not enough to prevent the rest of the Twelve from leaping into the fray, because they want to be the greatest as well. One more time, Jesus repeats His lesson about humility, servanthood, and sacrifice being the marks of greatness in the Kingdom (MARK 10:42–45).

Not until after the resurrection do Peter and the others understand both crosses. Peter preaches about the first cross at Pentecost (ACTS 3:18) and writes about the second cross eloquently in 1 PETER 2:21: "For you have been called for this purpose, since Christ also suffered for you, leaving you an example for you to follow in His steps." He continues in the same vein in 1 PETER 4:12–13: "Beloved, do not be surprised at the fiery ordeal among you, which comes upon you for your testing, as though some strange thing were happening to you; but to the degree that you share the sufferings of Christ, keep on rejoicing, so that also at the revelation of His glory you may rejoice with exultation."

Unless we recognize both crosses when we speak, it is probably better that we not speak at all. If we omit either His cross or our cross, we are not accurately representing the gospel of the Kingdom. We are called to suffer, and we identify with Christ through our suffering. Glory and honor in abundance will come our way for all eternity, but there is no shortcut. While Jesus was tempted in the desert (MATTHEW 4:1–10), Satan offered

Him a series of shortcuts. Jesus rejected them, choosing instead to walk the path of the cross that the Father had marked out for Him. We must do the same.

As I observe Jesus' patience with the Twelve over the course of MARK 8–10, I shake my head in wonder at their slowness to comprehend. Then I consider myself. I have had decades to learn elementary lessons that I have not yet mastered. I have had so many advantages. I have access to Scripture and many other spiritual resources. I grew up in a godly family. I have interacted with many mature saints. And yet I still have much growing to do. Jesus is indeed patient. I need to be equally patient with others.

We live in an upside-down Kingdom. We need to keep our eyes on eternal realities, not on earthly shadows or momentary and light afflictions. That is what we can expect when we're walking by the Spirit. If we're preoccupied by other concerns, we are on the wrong path. The correct path is marked by sacrifice and service rather than glory and ease.

Amy Carmichael, a famous missionary to India, wrote in *Candles in the Dark*, "A cup brimful of sweetness cannot spill even one drop of bitter water, no matter how suddenly jarred." I hate that statement, not because it's untrue, but because it *is* true, and very convicting.

Carmichael also captured the idea of the second cross wonderfully in her poem "Hast Thou No Scar":

Hast thou no scar?

No hidden scar on foot, or side, or hand?

I hear thee sung as mighty in the land,

I hear them hail thy bright ascendant star,

Hast thou no scar?

Hast thou no wound?

Yet, I was wounded by the archers, spent.

Leaned me against the tree to die, and rent

By ravening beasts that compassed me, I swooned:

Hast thou no wound?

No wound? No scar?

Yet as the Master shall the servant be,

And pierced are the feet that follow Me;

But thine are whole. Can he have followed far

Who has no wound nor scar?

For most people, this is not a natural attitude. I once encountered an exception, however. I was on a trip with a young man shortly after his conversion. He was one of the first people to come to the Lord from among the previously unengaged people group with whom my wife and I were living as missionaries. In the course of our conversation, I asked him what had convinced him to follow the Lord. His reply shocked me: "I looked around at all the pain and suffering and sorrow and evil in the world and determined that only a completely infinite and wise God could make sense of it all. You told me about that God." He was not running away from suffering; he was running to God and embracing the call to suffering. That insight could have been revealed to him only by the Lord. That recognition is a daily part of a life of Theopraxy.

If we trust the Lord as a faithful Creator and do what is right (1 PETER 4:19); if we have eternity in view as we walk through the troubles of this life (2 CORINTHIANS 4:17); if we trust that He will work out everything for His glory and our good (ROMANS 8:28)—then these convictions will impact our emotions and our responses as we (or those we love) face difficulty. We can respond with relative equanimity because we are viewing things from an eternal perspective.

Jesus wept upon Lazarus's death (JOHN 11:35), but it was not a grief without hope. As Paul contemplated death, he could confidently assert, "For to me, to live is Christ and to die is gain" (PHILIPPIANS 1:21). We know how the story ends, and any setback or sorrow is colored by that knowledge. That assurance enables us to be imperturbable in our core in the face of earthly troubles. *It is not that we feel less deeply, but that we feel more deeply. We have contemplated eternal emotions that render earthly ones pale by comparison.*

The same is true for the other side of the emotional ledger. I am certainly not a naturally happy-go-lucky or frivolous personality. My innate bent is toward Eeyore. Happily, the Lord has been dealing with my tendency toward a grim outlook. My joy has been increasing as I have learned to live in Theopraxy.

In recent years, perhaps the most frequent question I ask when checking in with those whom I am mentoring is "Are you having fun?" *I have discovered that the "fun factor" may be the best indicator of whether a person is living a Theopraxic life. It reveals whether a person is empowered by the Holy Spirit rather than his or her own efforts.*

The fun factor shows whether a person is trusting the Lord and has confidence in how things will turn out, or even an interested curiosity or humorous inquisitiveness about how the Lord will use some particularly difficult circumstances for His glory and our good in eternity. Fun, in this sense, is an evidence of living the abundant life that Jesus came to give us (JOHN 10:10).

Of course, a Theopraxic life is not all fun and games. In Scripture, God Himself expresses a range of emotions, including anger, frustration, yearning, jealousy, outrage, and irritation. If we are in tune with His thoughts and emotions, we will sense these with Him, but it will be in a righteous manner and for the right reasons—because we are upset when people pervert God's design and intentions and neglect His glory.

But Jesus was not a gloomy man. In fact, he was known as a partygoer (LUKE 7:34). People (except the Jewish religious leaders) enjoyed being around Him. Even in the Old Testament, God gave detailed instructions on how to celebrate, hold feasts, and have a good time. He expresses love, joy, and a sense of humor. Asking "Are you having fun?" reminds me to stay in tune with that aspect of God's heart and nature.

God has one all-consuming passion: His glory. He wants His glory to be experienced, reflected, and proclaimed by His creation, and most especially by mankind. All His other emotions are expressions or derivatives of this overriding passion. Remembering this truth gives me a reliable guide to evaluate my own emotional responses to situations I encounter. Even in His surprising twists and turns, I can best make sense of things when I evaluate the situation in terms of His glory.

PRAYER

Lord, I know You love me. But my comfort is not Your highest priority. To You, my goodness, Your Kingdom, and Your glory are more important. The truth is, I like comfort; but I love You more (at least, I want to love You more). Teach me to share Your perspective. Life is short and eternity is long. Earthly difficulties are light and momentary when compared to the joy of knowing You and the glory of being with You forever. Teach me to willingly take up my cross and follow You on the path of humility, sacrifice, and suffering—so that I might walk with You, experience the power of Your resurrection at work in my life, and know You now and forever.

QUESTIONS

Read the following questions, then pray and ask God what He wants you to learn and do. Listen quietly.

Review your journal. Are there any past commitments you have not completed? If needed, schedule revised completion dates.

1. Have I fully recognized not only the necessity of Jesus' cross, but the necessity of mine as well? If not, how might this recognition change my attitude and response to suffering?

2. Is there a price or sacrifice I am shying away from (like the rich young ruler)?

3. When I explain the gospel, do I share both crosses?

4. What specific actions does God want me to take in response to this chapter? (Note them in your journal and schedule them in your calendar.)

5. With whom (at least one name) does God want me to share what I have learned?

Ask the Lord to enable you to follow through on these commitments and to prepare the hearts of those with whom you intend to share insights.

PART

2

CORPORATE
ASPECTS OF
THEOPRAXY

7 The New Covenant

As members of the new covenant family, our eternal relationship with God is based on Jesus' faithfulness and righteousness. Our ability to live lives pleasing to Him is based on His gracious work within us.

"Behold, days are coming," declares the Lord, "when I will make a new covenant with the house of Israel and with the house of Judah, not like the covenant which I made with their fathers in the day I took them by the hand to bring them out of the land of Egypt, My covenant which they broke, although I was a husband to them," declares the Lord. "But this is the covenant which I will make with the house of Israel after those days," declares the Lord, "I will put My law within them and on their heart I will write it; and I will be their God, and they shall be My people. They will not teach again, each man his neighbor and each man his brother, saying, 'Know the Lord,' for they will all know Me, from the least of them to the greatest of them," declares the Lord, "for I will forgive their iniquity, and their sin I will remember no more."

—JEREMIAH 31:31–34

A covenant is an agreement between two parties that defines their relationship. One way to view the Bible is as a series of covenants between God and men. God makes covenants with Noah (GENESIS 6:18; 9:9–17); Abraham/Abram) (GENESIS 15:18; 17:1–21); then Isaac and Jacob (as renewals of the Abrahamic covenant in GENESIS 26:2-5 and GENESIS 35:11-12); Moses (EXODUS 24:7-8); David (2 SAMUEL 7:8–17); then Solomon (as a renewal of the Davidic covenant in 1 KINGS 9:1-5). On some occasions, God's people renewed the covenant when they realized they had broken it. For example, both Josiah (2 KINGS 23:1–3; 2 CHRONICLES 34:31–32) and Jehoiada (2 CHRONICLES 23:16) renewed the covenant between God and Israel.

The relationship between God and His people is very different in the Old Testament (under the Mosaic covenant) and the New Testament (under the new covenant). In the Old Testament, God's name was considered too holy to even pronounce. There was a keen sense of separation between God and man. This idea was depicted in the tabernacle, and later in the temple, through the inaccessibility of the Holy of Holies, where the high priest was allowed to enter God's presence only once a year (HEBREWS 9:6–7).

The Mosaic covenant was focused on the ethnic people of Israel. Under the Mosaic covenant, Israel received God's covenant blessings only if they obeyed God. "All these blessings will come upon you and overtake you if you obey the Lord your God" (DEUTERONOMY 28:2). Conversely, if Israel disobeyed God, God promised curses. "But it shall come about, if you do not obey the Lord your God, to observe to do all His commandments and His statutes with which I charge you today, that all these curses will come upon you and overtake you" (DEUTERONOMY 28:15).

Toward the end of the Old Testament period, the Lord, through His prophets, foreshadowed a new covenant. This new covenant would be different than God's covenant with Moses. The new covenant is everlasting (ISAIAH 59:21; JEREMIAH 32:40; 50:5; EZEKIEL 16:60; 37:26). Under the new covenant, God promises to transform His people on the inside so that they that will draw near to Him.

> "But this is the covenant which I will make with the house of Israel after those days," declares the Lord, "I will put My law within them and on their heart I will write it; and I will be their God, and they shall be My people." (JEREMIAH 31:33)

> "Moreover, I will give you a new heart and put a new spirit within you; and I will remove the heart of stone from your flesh and give you a heart of flesh." (EZEKIEL 36:26; SEE ALSO EZEKIEL 11:19)

> "I will put the fear of Me in their hearts so that they will not turn away from Me." (JEREMIAH 32:40B)

And God promises to deal with sin Himself, once and for all time. "'For they will all know Me, from the least of them to the greatest of them,' declares the Lord, 'for I will forgive their iniquity, and their sin I will remember no more'" (JEREMIAH 31:34B).

Why would there be a need for a new covenant? In short, both the scope and the basis of the old covenant needed to be strengthened. The Abrahamic and Mosaic covenants are the two major covenants that shape the Old Testament (if we consider the Davidic covenant as a continuation of the Abrahamic covenant). The Mosaic covenant is focused on Israel. From God's perspective, the Abrahamic covenant is still in effect (GALATIANS 3:16–18), with the entire world in view. God's promise to Abraham in GENESIS 12:1–3 included the promise that through him "all the families of the earth will be blessed." This is fully explained in GALATIANS 3:6–14. From a human perspective, however, the Abrahamic covenant was often limited to the physical descendants of Abraham (ROMANS 9:3–8). This limited understanding of the scope was problematic. This problem was rectified in the new covenant (ROMANS 4:1–25; GALATIANS 3:26–29), which is clearly universal.

NO IT WAS FOR A DIFFERENT PURPOSE

The Mosaic covenant was insufficient because of its basis. It was based, in part, on the obedience of God's people. Time after time, they demonstrated that they were incapable of fulfilling the requirements of God's law. Provision was made to deal with this unfaithfulness through animal sacrifices. This solution, however, was temporary and ultimately ineffective (HEBREWS 9:6–14). The new covenant is based on the faithfulness and righteousness of Christ. It is sealed by His blood (MATTHEW 26:28; MARK 14:24; LUKE 22:20; 1 CORINTHIANS 11:25). Further, under the promised new covenant, God vows to change His people from the inside out, giving them new hearts.

Given the sinfulness of our nature, the old covenant could never be sufficient. External law, no matter how true and good, could never lead us to obedience. It could never transform our inner selves. God, of course, knew this. He did not establish the Mosaic covenant in vain hope that we, with proper guidance, might change ourselves. God's purpose in establishing the Mosaic covenant was to make us see our need for grace, our need for a new covenant based on faith rather than earning salvation through our works (GALATIANS 3:19–29). "Therefore the Law has become our tutor to lead us to Christ, so that we may be justified by faith" (GALATIANS 3:24).

In the new covenant, God did what we could never do for ourselves:

> For what the Law could not do, weak as it was through the flesh, God did:
> sending His own Son in the likeness of sinful flesh and as an offering for
> sin, He condemned sin in the flesh, so that the requirement of the Law
> might be fulfilled in us, who do not walk according to the flesh but
> according to the Spirit. (ROMANS 8:3–4)

The Abrahamic covenant had a sign that accompanied it: circumcision.
The new covenant analog is baptism (COLOSSIANS 2:9–12). Baptism is our
formal acceptance of the promise and provision of God through Christ.
Just as circumcision was a demonstration of Abraham's obedience to
God's command (GENESIS 17:1–14, 23–27), so baptism is for us as well
(MATTHEW 28:18–20).

The Mosaic covenant was characterized by repeated sacrifices. The new
covenant is characterized by one sacrifice for all time, but one that we
remember each time we observe the Lord's Supper (LUKE 22:19–20; 1
CORINTHIANS 11:23–26). It serves as a reminder of the source of our life,
individually and corporately.

As New Testament believers, our relationship with God is very different
than was the case for God's people in the Old Testament. We are called
the Lord's friends (JOHN 15:15), and we can familiarly call the Father
"Daddy" (ROMANS 8:15; GALATIANS 4:6). Jesus is not ashamed to call us
his brothers and sisters (HEBREWS 2:11). The veil excluding us from the
Holy of Holies was literally torn apart when Jesus died (MATTHEW 27:51).
The new covenant was not limited to ethnic Israel, but was aimed at "all
the nations" (MATTHEW 28:19). And the blessings of the new covenant are
not earned by obedience, but are freely given, despite our lack of merit, "by
grace ... through faith ... not as a result of works" (EPHESIANS 2:8–9). The
new covenant is based not on law but on the Spirit (2 CORINTHIANS 3:4–6).
We are not bound by rules, but we are free to be transformed by the Spirit
into the likeness of the Lord as we come to see Him clearly (2 CORINTHIANS
3:17–18). This is a wonderful description of the life of Theopraxy.

All the covenants were corporate in nature. They did not define the
relationship between God and an individual, but between God and
His people. The new covenant is also corporate in nature (EPHESIANS
2:11–22). We are "no longer strangers and aliens, but ... fellow citizens
with the saints" and members of "God's household" (EPHESIANS 2:19).
Disciples from every tribe, language, and nation are now joining the

Jewish people in forming a living temple for the Lord. "For you once were not a people, but now you are the people of God" (1 PETER 2:10). All earthly distinctions are erased as we find our common identity and value in Christ (GALATIANS 3:26–29). His identity and value are central. Corporately we express His glory.

The book of Hebrews contrasts the old and new covenants. The author describes that contrast and tells us how we should live as a result. In HEBREWS 8:1–10:18, this contrast reaches its crescendo. The new covenant is personal rather than mediated, spiritual rather than external, and fixed (based on Jesus' performance) rather than changeable (based on our performance).

The author then summarizes what our appropriate response should be: to hold firmly to our faith in purity and encourage one another in that faith (HEBREWS 10:19–25). We should also endure through suffering (10:32–39).

In Chapter 11, the author then gives us Old Testament examples of this life of faith. He then presents Jesus as the ultimate example in HEBREWS 12:1–3:

> Therefore, since we have so great a cloud of witnesses surrounding us, let us also lay aside every encumbrance and the sin which so easily entangles us, and let us run with endurance the race that is set before us, fixing our eyes on Jesus, the author and perfecter of faith, who for the joy set before Him endured the cross, despising the shame, and has sat down at the right hand of the throne of God.
>
> For consider Him who has endured such hostility by sinners against Himself, so that you will not grow weary and lose heart.

The rest of the chapter expands on the theme of persevering through difficulties. It speaks of our response to discipline (HEBREWS 12:4–11), supporting and strengthening the weak (12:12–13), and responding to challenges in peace rather than bitterness or immorality (12:14–17). Finally, the chapter closes with an encouragement to persevere in obedience in even the most turbulent circumstances (12:18–29).

Chapter 13 focuses on relationships and character that are appropriate given the nature of our new covenant relationship with the Lord. We are to love our fellow believers (HEBREWS 13:1), show hospitality to strangers (13:2), support prisoners and those who are suffering (13:3), be faithful to and honor our spouses (13:4), and be free from the love of money

(13:5–6). We are to imitate godly leaders (13:7), suffer for the Lord, and live for our future with Him (13:12–14). We are to be grateful (13:15) and share sacrificially with others (13:16). All this sounds very similar to the descriptions of abiding in Christ, walking in the Spirit, or equivalent terms.

The difference between the new and old covenants is not the desired lifestyle or character of God's people, but the source and motivation for that life. The new covenant is maintained not by our performance, but by Jesus' performance. It is not lived by our power and ability, but by the indwelling Holy Spirit. It is not motivated by fear of losing our relationship with God, but by our gratitude for the grace He has given us. It is not something we are trying to avoid losing, but something we are eagerly growing into as the Lord draws us ever closer to His heart.

Ezekiel described the coming new covenant as the difference between having a heart of stone and a heart of flesh (EZEKIEL 11:19; 36:26). God's gift of this new heart is at the core of the new covenant. Both of these covenants are given in a corporate context. This relationship we hold in common is a key part of our corporate life in Christ. If God is our Father, then our fellow disciples are our brothers and sisters. This family relationship defines our interactions. Our family heritage defines us.

PRAYER

Father in heaven. Let me say that again—my Father in heaven. Thank You for the new covenant. You have dealt with our sin, once and for all. I need not fear. You have sent Your Spirit to live in us and make us new. We are freed from the law of sin and death and free to follow You by Your Spirit. You have made us Your people forever. We weren't a people; now we are. We are Your people. You are our Father, and we are brothers and sisters in You. Help us to step into what You have done.

QUESTIONS

Read the following questions, then pray and ask God what He wants you to learn and do. Listen quietly.

Review your journal. Are there any past commitments you have not completed? If needed, schedule revised completion dates.

1. Am I living and thinking as if I am still living in the old covenant? If so, in what respect?

2. How can I help others to better understand the wonderful realities of the new covenant?

3. How consistently is the source of my power for living rooted in God's grace rather than my own performance?

4. How consistently is the motivation for my spiritual life based in gratitude rather than in fear of not measuring up?

5. What specific actions does God want me to take in response to this chapter? (Note them in your journal and schedule them in your calendar.)

6. With whom (at least one name) does God want me to share what I have learned?

Ask the Lord to enable you to follow through on these commitments and to prepare the hearts of those with whom you intend to share insights.

8 The New Commandment

Love is the defining characteristic of Theopraxy.

A new commandment I give to you, that you love one another, even as I have loved you, that you also love one another. By this all men will know that you are My disciples, if you have love for one another.

—JOHN 13:34–35

Love is the one characteristic that most defines the life of Theopraxy: love for God and love for people, particularly the family of faith. Jesus summarized all of God's Old Testament commands in two: Love God and love others (MATTHEW 22:34–40). Further, on the night of His arrest, when He established the new covenant (MATTHEW 26:28; MARK 14:24; LUKE 22:20), He also gave His followers His new commandment (JOHN 13:34): ". . . love one another, even as I have loved you." People sometimes miss this connection because the new covenant is mentioned only in the Synoptic Gospels (i.e., Matthew, Mark, and Luke) and the new commandment only in John. John reiterates this message in his later writings (1 JOHN 2:7–8; 2 JOHN 5).

In JOHN 13, Jesus demonstrates His love to his disciples, then commands them to do the same for each other. The story starts by explaining what is going through Jesus' mind: "Jesus knowing that His hour had come that He would depart out of this world to the Father, having loved His own who were in the world, He loved them to the end" (13:1).

Jesus knew that His time on earth was ending, so He spent His last remaining hours loving His followers. Then, He gave them a demonstration. He took off his robe, wrapped a towel around himself, and washed their feet (13:4–11). Afterwards, He explained: "'Do you know what I have done to you? You call Me Teacher and Lord; and you are right, for *so I am*. If I then, the Lord and the Teacher, washed your feet, you also ought to wash one another's feet. For I gave you an example that you also should do as I did to you" (13:12B–15). Jesus was showing them not just how much He loved them, but also how they should love each other.

As they continued with their meal, Jesus explained that one of them sitting at that very table would betray Him and that He (Jesus) would be leaving them very soon. Then He gave them a command: "A new commandment I give to you, that you love one another, even as I have loved you, that you also love one another. By this all men will know that you are My disciples, if you have love for one another" (JOHN 13:34–35).

This new commandment is similar to the Old Testament version, but with additional emphases. It focuses on loving "one another"—other members of God's family. It gives an example or standard: We are to love each other as Jesus loves us. And the new commandment explains the result of obedience: This love, Jesus says in verse 35, will be the evidence that we are His disciples. Our love for each other shows the world that we follow Jesus.

This is both astonishing and frightening. Astonishing because, looking at the church today, we would not guess it; frightening because we often fall short of loving as Jesus loved. Yes, I love those who are easily lovable. But even pagans do that (MATTHEW 5:43–48). Nevertheless, our love for each other is meant to be the indicator demonstrating that we truly are Jesus' disciples. That demands our undivided attention. It has massive implications for our functioning within the church and for evangelism. Love is where the entire experience of Theopraxy comes into sharp focus.

? Only by the enablement of the Holy Spirit can we can love each other as Jesus loves us. This is true of the entire life of Theopraxy, but it is particularly true here. The Old Testament commands to love God and neighbor were already beyond our ability in our own strength. The new commandment goes farther, requiring us to love one another as Jesus loves us. The day He gave this command, Jesus was betrayed by one of the followers whose feet He had washed. The next day He was crucified. This demonstrates the degree of love He was commanding.

Later on during the evening when Jesus gave His new commandment, He explained more about love and unity in His high priestly prayer, recorded in JOHN 17:1–26. In VERSE 26 He explained that God's love will be in us, as His followers. "I have made Your name known to them, and will make it known, so that the love with which You loved Me may be in them, and I in them." Jesus called for the practical demonstration of that love as He prayed for unity among His follower:

> I do not ask on behalf of these alone, but for those also who believe in Me through their word; that they may all be one; even as You, Father, *are* in Me and I in You, that they also may be in Us, so that the world may believe that You sent Me.

> The glory which You have given Me I have given to them, that they may be one, just as We are one; I in them and You in Me, that they may be perfected in unity, so that the world may know that You sent Me, and loved them, even as You have loved Me.

> —JOHN 17:20–23

Wow. All of us who follow Jesus are to have the same degree of unity as the members of the Trinity! This comparison is repeated for emphasis in this passage. And our love for each other will serve as a testimony to the unbelieving world—in this case, "so that the world may know that You sent Me, and loved them, even as You have loved Me" (JOHN 17:23).

Perhaps one reason for our anemic evangelistic fruit is our failure to demonstrate love and unity within the body of Christ. After all, we have the best news imaginable—that it is possible to know, love, and serve the magnificent Lord of creation for all eternity. Unfortunately, in our actions toward one another, we often do not act as if this were true. Our failure to corporately live a life of thorough Theopraxy is a hindrance discouraging others from following Christ.

Jesus gave the new commandment and the new covenant at the same meal—the Last Supper, where He celebrated the Passover just prior to His betrayal and arrest. Before the supper, Jesus washed the disciples' feet as an expression of His love and service to them, and He directed them to serve one another just as He had served them. At that same meal, and around that same table, the disciples began to argue about which of them was the greatest, leading Jesus to remind them that in His Kingdom the greatest would be one who serves (LUKE 22:24–27).

In his commentary on Galatians, the fourth-century church father Jerome tells a story about the apostle John that had been passed down orally. When John was very old and infirm, he would be carried from place to place to speak. His message was always the same: "Children, love one another." When asked why his message never varied, he replied, "It is the Lord's command, and if it is done, it is enough."

John's writings constantly remind us to love one another (JOHN 13:34–35; 15:12, 17; 1 JOHN 3:11, 23; 4:7, 11–12; 2 JOHN 5). Paul mentions this command often too (ROMANS 12:10; 13:8; GALATIANS 5:13; EPHESIANS 4:2; 1 THESSALONIANS 3:12; 4:9; 2 THESSALONIANS 1:3), as does Peter (1 PETER 1:22; 4:8; 5:14).

Perhaps the best practical test of our mutual love is our finances. It is amazing how quickly we can slip into non-Kingdom priorities rather than being sacrificial with our money. This is not only true of individuals, but also of many congregations and their budgeting priorities. Like the rich young ruler, many people go away sad when they hear the Lord speaking with them about giving away money (LUKE 18:18–27). Like the Pharisees, they scoff at the idea that genuine faith should lead to generosity (LUKE 16:10–15).

Conversely, I have witnessed amazing selflessness and generosity on the part of some people, which provides a clear evidence that their commitment to the Lord is not merely mental assent. They are sanctified entirely, including their wallets.

One interesting manifestation of this generosity is a phenomenon that seems to be spontaneously appearing more and more frequently in pockets around the world. Some refer to it as base camps. There are a variety of expressions, but the salient characteristics include some degree of joint finances and economic activity akin to the shared resources of the early church in ACTS 2:44–45 and ACTS 4:32.

These base camps serve as ministry and equipping centers for making disciples and producing physical blessings. They model joint service toward the communities or regions where they are located. In so doing, they demonstrate corporate examples of selfless sacrifice and love for one another and the communities around them. In his book *Rising Tides*, Neil Cole describes these base camps, which he refers to as "Kingdom outposts," in greater detail. Several of the earliest examples I am aware of came out of the "listening group" discussed in the next chapter. Neil and I were two of the twelve participants in that group.

Love is the central theme of our life in Christ. It is the flavor or aroma that defines us. Love is easy to talk about but far more difficult to put into practice. The parable of the good Samaritan is instructive. There, an expert in the religious law asks Jesus, "Teacher, what shall I do to inherit eternal life?" (LUKE 10:25).

Jesus responds with a question: "What is written in the Law? How does it read to you?" (10:26).

The lawyer responds by quoting the Old Testament command to love God and love your neighbor (10:27). Jesus replies, "You have answered correctly; do this and you will live" (10:28).

But the lawyer is not satisfied with Jesus' affirmation. Instead, "wishing to justify himself, he said to Jesus, 'And who is my neighbor?'" (10:29). The religious lawyer wants a legal definition. In other words, he is asking, "Whom must I love and whom am I free not to love?"

Jesus responds with the familiar tale of the good Samaritan who crosses boundaries of hatred, race, and religion to help the Jewish man who has been robbed and beaten (10:30–37).

In the parable, the religious leaders who passed by the robbery victim were busy people with things to do. Stopping to care for an injured man would have created many inconveniences for them. But this account sounds remarkably similar to Jesus' story of the sheep and goats in MATTHEW 25:31–46. There Jesus declares that, on judgment day, He will welcome some into His Kingdom, saying, "Come, you who are blessed of My Father, inherit the kingdom prepared for you from the foundation of the world. For I was hungry, and you gave Me *something to eat; I was thirsty, and you gave Me something to drink; I was a stranger, and you invited Me in;* naked, and you clothed Me; I was sick, and you visited Me; I was in prison, and you came to Me" (25:34–36).

The people will reply in surprise, "Lord, when did we see You" and do any of those things (25:37–39)? Jesus will reply, "To the extent that you did it to one of these brothers of Mine, *even the least of them,* you did it to Me" (25:40).

Conversely, to others Jesus will say, "Depart from Me, accursed ones, into the eternal fire which has been prepared for the devil and his angels; for I was hungry, and you gave Me *nothing to eat; I was thirsty, and you gave Me nothing to drink;* I was a stranger, and you did not invite Me in; naked, and you did not clothe Me; sick, and in prison, and you did not visit Me" (MATTHEW 25:41–43).

Again, they will ask in surprise, "Lord, when did we see you . . . ?" (25:44). And Jesus will respond, "To the extent that you did not do it to one of the least of these, you did not do it to Me" (25:45).

From this passage, two things are inescapably clear. First, Jesus takes it very personally when we show (or fail to show) kindness "to one of these brothers of Mine" (25:40). He sees it as if we had treated Jesus Himself in that way. Second, the way we treat others is connected with how the Lord will treat us. Jesus made a similar comment in Matthew 6:14–15: "For if you forgive others for their transgressions, your heavenly Father will also forgive you. But if you do not forgive others, then your Father will not forgive your transgressions."

Those who demonstrate love in practical ways to the hungry, the thirsty, and people in need or in prison are those who enter God's Kingdom. Many people have lived lives of love, like the good Samaritan; many others have settled for making excuses, like the religious lawyer who tried to justify himself, eliciting Jesus' parable.

As John, the beloved disciple, expresses it: "Beloved, let us love one another, for love is from God; and everyone who loves is born of God and knows God. The one who does not love does not know God, for God is love" (1 JOHN 4:7–8).

Of course, we do not earn salvation by being kind to others. But our kindness toward others—especially our Christian brothers and sisters—is evidence that we are saved. Our love for one another proves that we are Jesus' disciples (JOHN 13:35). Our unity proves that the Father sent Jesus (JOHN 17:21, 23) and that He loves us (JOHN 17:23).

Like the Corinthians, we can be impressed by people with strong spiritual gifts. We admire eloquent speakers, people of great faith or amazing insights, those who have done great works or appear to have tremendous fruit in their ministry. We have a celebrity culture. Those achievements are good things, but love is a great thing (1 CORINTHIANS 12:31). In fact, without love, all those things are utterly meaningless (1 CORINTHIANS 13:1–3, 8–10). Mother Teresa said it well: "Not all of us can do great things. But we can do small things with great love."

God is less concerned with the size of our actions than with the love with which we do them. I frequently tell people I am mentoring, "You be concerned with the depth of your ministry and God will take care of the breadth of your ministry." I learned this from one of my own mentors, Bill Smith. It expresses the concept of the spiritual economy of Matthew 10:8 (Freely you have received; freely give) and of LUKE 16:10 (If you are faithful in little, you will be faithful in much).

This truth is comforting, because we will be judged by our faithfulness in using what we have, not by the size of our gifts. God evaluates us based on our hearts, not our achievement. After seeing rich people making large gifts to the temple, and a poor widow dropping in two small copper coins, Jesus said, "Truly I say to you, this poor widow put in more than all *of them*; for they all out of their surplus put into the offering; but she out of her poverty put in all that she had to live on" (LUKE 21:3–4). In God's eyes, her gift was larger than theirs, because her small gift was, for her, a large sacrifice—demonstrating a heart of faith and love.

The same principle applies in many areas of life. I am by nature a hyper-introvert with relatively weak interpersonal skills. When I see someone with excellent people skills, I often think, "It would be great to have people skills like that." My own personality makes me poorly suited for any sort of public ministry role. But I can take comfort that my ministry efforts—although uncomfortable for me and perhaps considered meager or even pitiable by others—are noticed and even honored by the Lord. He recognizes them as a sacrifice of service and love.

This pattern of showing our love out of our inadequacy also results in God demonstrating His power by working through us despite our weaknesses (1 CORINTHIANS 1:27; 2 CORINTHIANS 12:10). It has the added benefit of helping us not to be proud or do things in our own strength.

In sum, love is the primary characteristic of the Theopraxic life: love for God and love for people. Jesus, in His new commandment, gave special priority to loving those in the family of faith. The reality of this love is demonstrated (or disproved) by practical action to help those in need. As Paul says in GALATIANS 6:10, "Let us do good to all people, and especially to those who are of the household of the faith."

Our love for each other tells the world that we are Jesus' disciples and that Jesus is really from the Father. Of course, we cannot fix every problem for every person. But we can help someone with something. God, who sees all, will evaluate us not based on the size of what we do, but based on our hearts of love and sacrifice.

PRAYER

Father in heaven, the Bible says You are love. And You want us to be the same toward You and toward people (especially toward my Christian brothers and sisters). This makes me nervous. Like the religious lawyer in the story of the good Samaritan, I want to limit my duty to love. But you reject those limits. Help me to pour out my life for others as You did for me. I can afford it because You are with me. Change me from selfish to loving—like You. Change my heart and change my actions. I pray in Jesus' name.

QUESTIONS

Read the following questions, then pray and ask God what He wants you to learn and do. Listen quietly.

Review your journal. Are there any past commitments you have not completed? If needed, schedule revised completion dates.

1. How much time, energy, and money do I spend practically loving those in need?

2. Do I treat other believers in a way that causes people to think, "Wow, he/she really is a follower of Jesus!" If so, how? If not, where am I falling short?

3. Would other people describe my life as embodying the characteristics mentioned in 1 Corinthians 13:4-7? Why or why not?

4. What specific actions does God want me to take in response to this chapter? (Note them in your journal and schedule them in your calendar.)

5. With whom (at least one name) does God want me to share what I have learned?

Ask the Lord to enable you to follow through on these commitments and to prepare the hearts of those with whom you intend to share insights.

9 Listening to God Together

Listening to the Lord is important not only from an individual perspective but also from a corporate standpoint.

For just as we have many members in one body and all the members do not have the same function, so we, who are many, are one body in Christ, and individually members one of another.

—ROMANS 12:4–5

But one and the same Spirit works all these things, distributing to each one individually just as He wills. For even as the body is one and yet has many members, and all the members of the body, though they are many, are one body, so also is Christ.

—I CORINTHIANS 12:11–12

Listening to God is important not only at the individual level but also at the corporate level. Because the Lord speaks to each of us differently and has made each of us unique, the result is not uniformity but unity.

First Corinthians 2 is quite relevant to the matter of achieving unity. It describes the solution to the problem that arose when believers wanted to follow their favorite human teacher (Paul or Apollos or Cephas) rather than God.

From I CORINTHIANS 2:6 through the end of CHAPTER 2, Paul speaks in the first person plural. "We" speak wisdom from God (2:6–9) by the Holy Spirit (2:10–13). Those who are not in the Spirit cannot understand it (2:8, 14–16). He concludes that "we have the mind of Christ." I believe the plural is significant. Just as the parts of the body are interdependent, so it is in our relating to our Head, Jesus Christ, and having the mind of Christ. God does not reveal His whole purpose to any one individual. We need one another.

At the very least, this common source of our guidance implies a unity or consistency that comes from hearing the same voice. It also implies a degree of coordination or compatibility. I would suggest that one way to more fully achieve this in a practical way is to be intentional about listening corporately.

Because of my cultural background and personality, this has been a difficult lesson for me to learn. I am accustomed to listening to God and making decisions by myself. That is most comfortable for me. But it is not necessarily best. Sometimes it is better to involve other brothers and sisters in the process.

One practical pattern that has helped me has been "listening groups." In the 2000s, about a dozen of us would meet for a few days every six months or so for the purpose of hearing from God together. We would listen individually for a period of time (a half hour or an hour) and then gather to share what we had heard and determine how those messages intersected and connected. We would go through that cycle repeatedly over the course of our few days together.

At first our efforts were a bit awkward, but over time we came to know one another better and trust one another more. Some significant ministry resulted from our times together. But for me, the greater work was to teach me to regularly listen to God together with others, then assemble the individual messages from the Lord into a coherent corporate message.

This basic approach can be applied in a variety of contexts. It does not have to be preplanned multiday events. It can be a "spur of the moment" occurrence with two or more people. The key is for all participants to be disciples who are walking in the Spirit and who are seeking to know the Lord's will regarding direction or action in a situation in which each of them is involved. It can be formal or informal. It can involve people in organizations or simply friends or family. There should, however, be a degree of mutual commitment and direction.

The process reminds me of the story of the blind men who encountered an elephant for the first time. Each felt a different part of the elephant—

the trunk, the tail, a side, or a leg. One said, "An elephant is like a big snake." Another said, "An elephant is like a rope." Another said, "An elephant is like a wall." The last said, "An elephant is like a tree trunk." They were all accurately describing what they had felt. They were all right. But each one had a very different and very incomplete perspective on the nature of an elephant. If they pooled their observations, they could much more accurately describe an elephant.

I believe our hearing from God is similar. Because God is infinite and our understanding of Him is partial, and because each of us has a unique calling, gifting, and set of experiences, we gain a fuller understanding of His corporate messages to the body if we share with one another what each of us is hearing individually. In so doing, we gain a greater appreciation for one another's parts of the greater task and how we can collaborate and cooperate more effectively.

Not everyone's schedule or situation lends itself to this specific practice of a listening group, but anyone can apply the pattern. Any group of believers can listen to the Lord together in pursuit of corporate obedience and stewardship of the message He gives. Any group that needs to make corporate decisions can set aside time to listen and then share what they are hearing as a basis for moving forward, even if they don't meet together repeatedly or regularly.

Practicing such patterns proves difficult if the group is mixed—that is, if it includes some members who are abiding in Christ and some who are either not believers or not actively walking in the Spirit. For us to function effectively as the body of Christ, everyone needs to be trained in hearing the Lord and fully committed to obeying Him, whatever the risk or sacrifice may be. We need to trust one another.

This is why the injunctions against allying ourselves with those who do not belong to Christ (e.g., 2 CORINTHIANS 6:14–18) are so critical. We cannot function effectively as a divided group. This is also why Jesus' instructions on church discipline in MATTHEW 18:15–20 are essential, no matter how uncomfortable putting them into practice may be. We need to judge those who are within the church (1 CORINTHIANS 5:9–6:11).

When the whole body of Christ is walking in the Spirit and in unity, then we can hear the Lord corporately in ways that would never happen in isolation. We can hear aspects of His message to the church that become apparent only when we piece together the messages given to each of us.

This is the process I described with the listening group. Together, as the body of Christ, we march to the beat of a different drummer than does the world. Each of us in the body is playing a different instrument in the orchestra, even though we hear the same drummer. This is an important aspect of hearing God corporately.

Jesus illustrated this, using Himself and John the Baptist as an example:

> But to what shall I compare this generation? It is like children sitting in the market places, who call out to the other *children*, and say, "We played the flute for you, and you did not dance; we sang a dirge, and you did not mourn." For John came neither eating nor drinking, and they say, "He has a demon!" The Son of Man came eating and drinking, and they say, "Behold, a gluttonous man and a drunkard, a friend of tax collectors and sinners!" Yet wisdom is vindicated by her deeds.
>
> —MATTHEW 11:16–19

Both Jesus and John were hearing from the Lord and fulfilling God's design for them. Although their approach to ministry and their demeanors were strikingly different, both were "on the same page" in putting the focus on Jesus and the Kingdom of heaven. Their work was complementary, and they both understood and appreciated the contribution of the other.

? We also need to discern, sensitively but forthrightly, who is actually not in the Kingdom. We cannot listen to the Lord in unity with those who do not know Him and hear Him. This is a practical application of the command not to be "bound together with unbelievers" (2 CORINTHIANS 6:14–18). Jesus reserved His harshest words and most intense criticism for those who thought they were followers of God but were not (MATTHEW 23:1–39). He told them to their faces that they were not obeying God, and as evidence He cited their inability to hear God (JOHN 8:47).

This is uncomfortable for us, or at least I know it is for me. I need to remind myself that I am not doing anyone a favor by allowing them to continue in a state of false security. This requires clarity and discernment from the Lord, especially when dealing with people who are part of a church but not actually in the Kingdom.

Church discipline is rarely practiced in our congregations today. When it is practiced, it seems to be practiced only with regard to church staff and in the area of sexual sin. This is partly because there is virtually no accountability in place with church members, so we have no reliable way to stimulate them to obey and pass on to others what the Lord has been speaking to us. People listen to a sermon and then promptly forget what they heard. No one has them ask the Lord to personalize the principles they have heard. No one checks back with them to see how they have done. Communications are one-to-many rather than two-way conversations. As a result, we have no way of knowing whether fellow church members are actively sinning or not. ? ~ IS THAT OUR ROLE ?

Moreover, in the few cases when church discipline is practiced, the pattern that Jesus described, ending in the exclusion of the offending member if necessary (MATTHEW 18:15–17), is not followed, nor is Paul's exhortation in GALATIANS 6:1 about acting with the ultimate goal of restoration in mind. We should be concerned with and working toward helping every believer live a fully sanctified life. This is the most loving thing we can do for one another. That is why we need to hold one another accountable.

As for those who truly are in the Kingdom, we need to show more grace to one another. God demands unity, not uniformity. He has, by His own design and will, given us different roles, different tasks, different operating environments, different cultures, and different callings. He also speaks to each of us differently and gives us different portions of His truth and will. This is necessary so we can reach all types of people. We are not to judge ? the servant of another, and especially not God's servants (see ROMANS 14:1–23, especially VERSE 4).

At the Tower of Babel (GENESIS 11:1–9), the confusion of the languages was God's way of forcing compliance with His instructions to fill the earth (GENESIS 1:28; 9:1). As usual, what man intended for evil, God used for good. The end result was the creation of a variety of languages and cultures, each of which reveals variegated nuances of God's glory.

This same principle is reflected in the spiritual gifts God gives the body. It is also reflected in the patterns of listening groups, as each person contributes his or her unique aspect of the greater perspective. Each of us needs to understand the bigger picture in order that we might know God more fully.

People often assume that the goal of a listening group is to have everyone hear the same thing, and that consensus confirms the message. Sometimes that is the case, especially when a specific decision is required, such as at the Jerusalem council (ACTS 15). But these should not be the only times we are listening together.

When we look to the Lord corporately for His input as a matter of consistent conviction, we learn to put together the pieces of the puzzle as He gives a portion of His message to each person. We are not looking for each person to hear the same thing; rather, we are looking for how the Lord will involve each person in hearing and responding to His message. He wants us to seek and serve Him together. He wants us to need each other as we lean on Him and look to Him.

Some issues of core commitment or morality demand consistency among all believers, but many issues require multiple, complementary approaches. This helps make God's truth known in its multifaceted fullness. It enables us to play our individual parts in fulfilling God's will more effectively and with greater coordination. It helps us appreciate one another's contributions.

The bottom line with regard to corporately seeking the mind of Christ is illustrated by Joshua's experience just prior to the battle of Jericho, as recorded in JOSHUA 5:13–14:

> Now it came about when Joshua was by Jericho, that he lifted up his eyes and looked, and behold, a man was standing opposite him with his sword drawn in his hand, and Joshua went to him and said to him, "Are you for us or for our adversaries?" He said, "No; rather I indeed come now *as* captain of the host of the Lord." And Joshua fell on his face to the earth, and bowed down, and said to him, "What has my lord to say to his servant?"

This is the proper perspective. It is not a question of whether others are on "our side," but whether they are on God's side. If we are all truly on God's side, then we will all be in complete unity on a deep level. We will all exhibit the fruit of the Spirit. We will know God's priorities and display His character, including humility and servanthood. We will experience true mutual submission. We will all be listening to God and assembling what we hear into a coherent, comprehensive understanding of His will. In this way, we will experience the answer to Jesus' prayer in John 17, gaining the wisdom that only comes from having God's perspective (ISAIAH 55:9).

PRAYER

Lord, enable me to be in tune with You and with my brothers and sisters in Christ to the degree that we can hear You better together than I can alone. Let us then be able to fulfill Your will together in ways and to a degree that we cannot do so separately. Let us bring joy to Your heart and a testimony to the world in doing so.

QUESTIONS

Read the following questions, then pray and ask God what He wants you to learn and do. Listen quietly.

Review your journal. Are there any past commitments you have not completed? If needed, schedule revised completion dates.

1. Have I ever experienced corporate listening, not just to see if group members are hearing the same thing, but to assemble God's messages to individuals into a coherent whole? Whom might I ask to join me in such an experiment?

2. What specific actions does God want me to take in response to this chapter? (Note them in your journal and schedule them in your calendar.)

3. With whom (at least one name) does God want me to share what I have learned?

Ask the Lord to enable you to follow through on these commitments and to prepare the hearts of those with whom you intend to share insights.

10 The Trinity Is Our Model for Unity

As the Trinity is one, so we are to be one (if we live Theopraxically).

I do not ask on behalf of these alone, but for those also who believe in Me through their word; that they may all be one; even as You, Father, are in Me and I in You, that they also may be in Us, so that the world may believe that You sent Me.

The glory which You have given Me I have given to them, that they may be one, just as We are one; I in them and You in Me, that they may be perfected in unity, so that the world may know that You sent Me, and loved them, even as You have loved Me.

—JOHN 17:20–23

The Trinity is a mystery. The word itself seems a contradiction: tri-unity. At the beginning of the Bible narrative, when God refers to Himself in the plural (GENESIS 1:26: "Let Us make man in Our image, according to Our likeness"), we start to suspect that something strange is happening. We get more hints scattered throughout the Old Testament—various theophanies of the "angel of the Lord" along with references to the "Spirit of the Lord."

The Trinity becomes more explicit in the New Testament, in narrative accounts such as Jesus' baptism (MATTHEW 3:16–17) or the Great Commission (MATTHEW 28:19–20)—where Father, Son, and Spirit are all mentioned—and in the prayers of the epistles (e.g., 2 CORINTHIANS 13:14). But one of the most intriguing glimpses into the nature of the relationships within the Trinity comes from JOHN 17:20–26:

> I do not ask on behalf of these alone, but for those also who believe
> in Me through their word; that they may all be one; even as You,
> Father, *are in Me and I in You, that they also may be in Us, so that the
> world may believe that You sent Me.*
>
> *The glory which You have given Me I have given to them, that they
> may be one, just as We are one; I in them and You in Me, that they
> may be perfected in unity, so that the world may know that You sent
> Me, and loved them, even as You have loved Me.* Father, I desire
> that they also, whom You have given Me, be with Me where I am, so
> that they may see My glory which You have given Me, for You loved Me
> before the foundation of the world.
>
> O righteous Father, although the world has not known You, yet I have
> known You; and these have known that You sent Me; and I have made
> Your name known to them, and will make it known, so that the love
> with which You loved Me may be in them, and I in them.

The mutuality and unity described defy conventional logic. The Father is
in the Son and the Son is in the Father (JOHN 17:21). The Father and the
Son are one (17:22). The Father gives glory to the Son (17:22, 24).
The Father has loved the Son since before the foundation of the world
(17:24). The Son makes the Father's name known (17:26). Father and Son
are one, yet distinct. They exist in an eternal fellowship of unity, mutual
love, and mutual honor. Amazing!

Even more, Father and Son and Spirit invite us to join them in this mystery.
We are to be one as they are one (JOHN 17:21). We are to be in them as
they are in each other (17:21). The Son has given us the glory that the
Father gave to Him, so that we can be one as they are one (17:22). The
Son is in us as the Father is in Him, so that we can be "perfected in unity"
(17:23). Tenderly, the Son wants us to be with Him, where He is, so that we
can see the glory the Father has given Him (17:24). Staggering!

It strains my imagination to think of that sort of unity among the persons
of the Godhead. It is even more difficult to imagine us sharing a similar
unity with the Trinity and with one another. This unity is possible because
of the Spirit. In JOHN 16:13–14, Jesus explains:

> But when He, the Spirit of truth, comes, He will guide you into all the
> truth; for He will not speak on His own initiative, but whatever He hears,
> He will speak; and He will disclose to you what is to come. He will glorify
> Me, for He will take of Mine and will disclose it to you.

The Spirit is our built-in translator and communications officer for constant interaction with the Trinity. This is the heart of Theopraxy. We cannot possibly be in tune with God and one another without being constantly attentive to God's thoughts and actions and desires through the Holy Spirit.

Ephesians 4 gives us a glimpse of how this plays out. Paul adjures his readers to "walk in a manner worthy of the calling with which you have been called" (EPHESIANS 4:1). This exhortation to walk worthy is yet another way of saying "walk in the Spirit," "abide in Christ," or be "filled with the Spirit." (Note that in verse 2 the worthy walk is characterized by the fruit of the Spirit—humility, gentleness, patience, and love).

Then Paul moves to his main point: unity. We are to be "diligent to preserve the unity of the Spirit in the bond of peace" (4:3). This unity stems from our identity: "There is one body and one Spirit, just as also you were called in one hope of your calling; one Lord, one faith, one baptism, one God and Father of all who is over all and through all and in all " (4:4–6). Given our common heritage, disunity contradicts our basic identity in Christ. It can occur only if we fail to walk in the Spirit, abide in Christ, or be filled with the Spirit and His fruit—in short, if we fail to live a life of Theopraxy.

Paul makes it clear that unity is not the same as uniformity. To the contrary, different members of the body are given different gifts (4:7–16), but all with the goal of building one body. Just as each member of the Trinity has a unique role, so it is in the body of Christ. We are to equip one another (4:12) so that we might all do the work of the Kingdom, build up the body, attain the unity of the faith and of the knowledge of the Son of God, and become mature and conformed to His image (4:13). This is meant to happen through mutual ministry as we speak the truth in love to one another (4:14–15). By so doing, Jesus holds us together as we work together and are thus built up in love (4:16).

Paul is not naïve. He knows unity is neither natural nor easy. He acknowledges that sin, selfishness, dishonesty, anger, resentment, and laziness stand in the way (4:17–28). Nonetheless, he exhorts us to be "diligent to preserve the unity of the Spirit in the bond of peace" (4:3).

Theopraxy is a team sport. When God adopts us as His children, we get a new Father. We also get new brothers and sisters. We cannot have a good relationship with our Father if we don't get along with our brothers and sisters. This is one of the fundamental themes of 1 John, written by "the disciple whom Jesus loved":

> 1 JOHN 2:9: *The one who says he is in the Light and yet hates his brother is in the darkness until now.*

> 1 JOHN 3:14: *We know that we have passed out of death into life, because we love the brethren. He who does not love abides in death.*

> 1 JOHN 3:17: *But whoever has the world's goods, and sees his brother in need and closes his heart against him, how does the love of God abide in him?*

> 1 JOHN 4:7–8: *Beloved, let us love one another, for love is from God; and everyone who loves is born of God and knows God. The one who does not love does not know God, for God is love.*

> 1 JOHN 4:11: *Beloved, if God so loved us, we also ought to love one another.*

> 1 JOHN 4:20: *If someone says, "I love God," and hates his brother, he is a liar; for the one who does not love his brother whom he has seen, cannot love God whom he has not seen.*

> 1 JOHN 4:21: *And this commandment we have from Him, that the one who loves God should love his brother also.*

> 1 JOHN 5:1: *Whoever believes that Jesus is the Christ is born of God, and whoever loves the Father loves the child born of Him.*

In these verses, John makes two basic points. First, God expects Christians to love each other, deeply and practically. Second, it is an inherent contradiction to love God and not love His children. If we think we love God, yet don't love His children, we are deceiving ourselves.

The reality of our relationship with the Father is demonstrated by how we treat His children. We absolutely require mutual interaction with our siblings in Christ to become mature and fruitful, to know God, and to become like Christ. ROMANS 12 and 1 CORINTHIANS 12 both address this point extensively.

Scripture highlights our corporate identity as the body of Christ hundreds of times. This is uncomfortable for me, as an individualistic American, and also because of my introverted personality. My natural bent is to be independent and focus on myself. I need to echo Paul in EPHESIANS 1:18, when he prays "that the eyes of your heart may be enlightened, so that you will know what is the hope of His calling, what are the riches of the glory of His inheritance in the saints." Viewing fellow believers in that way is not my natural inclination.

It is plain, from these and many other passages, that God's children ought to be unified. But the reality is that we are not. How should we respond to this disparity? The Bible gives some practical steps each of us can take.

First, we cannot simply throw up our hands and surrender. We have the duty to pursue unity with our brothers and sisters. Paul writes, for example:

> Now I exhort you, brethren, by the name of our Lord Jesus Christ, that you all agree and that there be no divisions among you, but that you be made complete in the same mind and in the same judgment. (1 CORINTHIANS 1:10; see also EPHESIANS 4:3, COLOSSIANS 3:14; ROMANS 15:5–6; PHILIPPIANS 1:27; 2:2; 1 PETER 3:8; 2 CORINTHIANS 13:11)

Paul wrote these words to a church that was deeply divided. They were split into factions, each following different leaders: "I am of Paul," "I am of Apollos," "I am of Cephas," or even "I am of Christ" (1 CORINTHIANS 1:12). He is well aware that they fall short of the ideal, but he still challenges them to pursue it.

Second, we pursue unity through self-sacrifice. In PHILIPPIANS 2:1–11, Paul explains that unity is achieved through unselfishness. We are all in favor of unity, but we seek it by trying to get others to do things our way. Paul offers a different plan. He begins by emphasizing the foundation stones that all believers share: "encouragement in Christ, . . . consolation of love, . . . fellowship of the Spirit, . . . affection and compassion" (2:1). He then states the goal—unity: "being of the *same* mind, maintaining the *same* love, *united* in spirit, intent on *one purpose*" (2:2, emphasis added).

After stating the goal, Paul explains how to attain it. We attain unity not by persuading others to agree with us, but through unselfishness:

> Do nothing from selfishness or empty conceit, but with humility of mind regard one another as more important than yourselves; do not merely look out for your own personal interests, but also for the interests of others. (PHILIPPIANS 2:3–4)

Then Paul illustrates with an example—the example of Jesus. We should "have this attitude . . . which was also in Christ Jesus" (PHILIPPIANS 2:5). Jesus did not cling to His right to divine glory, "but emptied Himself, taking the form of a bond-servant" (PHILIPPIANS 2:7). Having come to earth as a man, He humbly obeyed the Father "by becoming obedient to the point of death, even death on a cross" (PHILIPPIANS 2:8). He sacrificed everything and suffered willingly for us, though we did not deserve it. As a consequence, "God highly exalted Him, and bestowed on Him the name which is above every name" (PHILIPPIANS 2:9).

This same unselfishness characterizes the Trinity as well. The Spirit glorifies Jesus (JOHN 16:13–14); Jesus glorifies the Father (JOHN 17:1); the Father glorifies the Son (JOHN 8:54). The Father will place all things under the Son's authority, and then the Son will give all to the Father (1 CORINTHIANS 15:24–28). We are to imitate this when we "give preference to one another in honor" (ROMANS 12:10).

Third, we move toward unity by honoring the differences between us. It is human nature to value the things we are good at. If we are athletic, we think it is important to be fit. If we are intelligent, we admire other intelligent people (and despise the less clever). If we are good-looking, articulate, hard-working, or organized, we tend to appreciate people who are like us. God looks at it differently. He deliberately made people different. He gave different people different gifts and abilities so that, together, we could be and accomplish what He desires. He made us to need each other.

> For the body is not one member, but many. If the foot says, "Because I am not a hand, I am not a part of the body," it is not for this reason any the less a part of the body. And if the ear says, "Because I am not an eye, I am not a part of the body," it is not for this reason any the less a part of the body. If the whole body were an eye, where would the hearing be? If the whole were hearing, where would the sense of smell be? But now God has placed the members, each one of them, in the body, just as He desired. (1 CORINTHIANS 12:14–18)

It is easy to be frustrated with people who are different. But God has put them there for us.

To preserve unity, we must focus on our own responsibilities, not on judging others. I have a keen eye to spot things that other people are doing wrong, and I want to tell them, or others, what I see. But that is not my job. ROMANS 14:4 is a useful corrective:

Who are you to judge the servant of another? To his own master he stands or falls; and he will stand, for the Lord is able to make him stand.

I am not the judge. God is. My brothers and sisters will not appear before me on judgment day. They will stand before God. And God, by His grace, is able to make them stand. When I feel the urge to criticize, I try to remind myself that I have enough difficulty fulfilling my own responsibilities to the Lord. I don't need to assume responsibility for anyone else. God is their judge, not me.

Further, I need to remember that, in matters of personal preference, mature believers let the other person have it their way. I observe that many of the quarrels within churches are about matters of preference: The music is too loud (or not loud enough); the sermon is too long (or not long enough). Why are we starting a Saturday night service? Why don't we have Wednesday night prayer meetings, or Awana, or MOPS anymore? None of these are matters of biblical principle. They are matters of perception or tradition or preference. In those matters, the mature believer should be willing to sacrifice his or her preference to maintain unity. The willingness to do so is a symptom of maturity.

This is the basic point of ROMANS 14. Paul is discussing debatable matters. Can you eat meat that is, or might have been, sacrificed to idols? On which days should we worship? Here is what Paul concludes:

> Therefore let us not judge one another anymore, but rather determine this—not to put an obstacle or a stumbling block in a brother's way.... . So then we pursue the things which make for peace and the building up of one another. (ROMANS 14:13, 19)

At its root, disunity is a function of sinfulness. The only real remedy is to live Theopraxically—to abide in Christ, to be filled with the Spirit, to keep in step with the Spirit. Remember, now we are corporately one with the Trinity. We see this truth not only in JOHN 15 and 17, but Paul reminds us of it in 1 CORINTHIANS 6:17: "The one who joins himself to the Lord is one spirit with Him." If this is the case, how can there be divisions among us?

Paul addresses this issue in 1 CORINTHIANS 1:10–13. This is the same Corinthian church to which Paul felt compelled to write about the proper use of spiritual gifts and about love. They were divided into factions based on what person they followed. Paul reminds them that Christ is not divided.

Then, in chapter 3, the apostle discusses the issue more completely. By having human allegiances that divided the body, he says that the Corinthians were "walking like mere men" (1 CORINTHIANS 3:3). He points out that each of the leaders they were following were servants of Christ. Christ, not the human leader, was ultimately responsible for any good thing that happened. Each person was playing his own role as called by Christ, and none could take credit for it. The quality of work matters, and each person will receive a reward based on that criterion, but everyone is to follow Christ alone.

> So then let no one boast in men. For all things belong to you, whether Paul or Apollos or Cephas or the world or life or death or things present or things to come; all things belong to you, and you belong to Christ; and Christ belongs to God. (1 CORINTHIANS 3:21–23)

The divisions experienced in the Corinthian church have their equivalents today in believers' preferences for a particular teacher, author, theologian, denomination, mission network, or ministry technique. There are practical reasons for structural divisions, of course, but not for the divisiveness and even enmity that have come to typify so many relationships within the larger body of Christ. Pride, envy, bitterness, distrust, and disdain have become all too common, especially where the church has become too comfortable and self-serving. It seems as if lines of separation are being drawn in ever smaller circles, preventing the spiritual unity that the Lord desires.

I fear that if this trend continues, we will become entirely an earthly kingdom of individuals. The problem is simple: We have forgotten the source of our unity. If we fail to abide in Christ the King, we cannot have the sort of unity He died for us to experience.

In JOHN 15, Jesus makes it abundantly clear that life in His Kingdom is possible only for those who abide in Him. We cannot bear fruit in any other way. In fact, we cannot do *anything* without abiding in Him (JOHN 15:4–5). Jesus describes various remarkable results and promises related to our abiding in Him. He also makes clear in JOHN 15:12–17 and again in JOHN 17:21 that our love for one another is integrally intertwined with our abiding in Him.

Being Theopraxic is therefore a prerequisite for achieving the unity that Jesus commanded and prayed for. But many obstacles can get in our way. One of the biggest hindrances in my mind is related to the pervasive concern for organizational survival. The larger a church or Christian organization becomes, the more dangerous this distraction is, as we are tempted to confuse the prosperity of our organization or church with that of the Kingdom of God.

There is a widespread assumption that the advance of God's Kingdom depends on the advance of various institutions, including individual churches. Thus, we rule out decisions or courses of action that might threaten our institutions. This attitude leads to organizational pragmatism rather than listening to the Lord. When we put our own organization's interests first, we cannot achieve Christian unity, which requires putting the interests of others (and of the Kingdom) ahead of our own. Acting based on the pragmatism of organizational survival and prosperity is a death knell to unity.

Due to the upside-down nature of the Kingdom, the Lord frequently asks us to do things that do not make sense from the perspective of organizational benefit. A willingness to embrace sacrifice, which we discussed earlier in an individual context, is equally necessary at the corporate level. *Sacrificing and dying are the bread and butter of living in the Kingdom. They are daily occurrences. This is true corporately as well as individually.*

Both as individuals and as organizations we need to follow the principle of MATTHEW 6:33. This verse concludes Jesus' conversation concerning focus and worry. He has discussed the things we tend to worry about—money, food, clothes, life itself. Then he says, "But seek first His Kingdom and His righteousness, and all these things will be added to you." This verse is an allocation of responsibilities. Jesus is saying that if we make it our job to pursue God's righteousness and God's Kingdom, God will make it His job to provide what we need. This principle applies to both organizations and individuals. Unity is impossible without this willingness to put God's Kingdom first.

One positive example of corporate sacrifice was Last Days Ministries, founded by Christian musician Keith Green. Long before electronic music distribution came along, back when giving music away was an expensive proposition, Last Days "sold" its music for whatever a person felt led to give. This resulted in vast quantities of free "sales," which continued even after Green's untimely death in a 1982 plane crash at age twenty-eight. Last Days was not in a position of financial strength. This approach to distribution appeared destined to kill the ministry from the very beginning, but Keith followed the leading of the Lord in this matter. His stance is the epitome of Kingdom-first priorities.

Keith Green made many people uncomfortable with his radical call to discipleship. But Christian unity does not mean just swallowing our differences in favor of a superficial "getting along." It means everyone pulling toward the same goal, in a way that encourages and challenges one another toward growing in Christ. Keith's sacrificial service without concern for financial gain was a great example of that spirit.

There are plenty of negative examples. One time I was training on disciple making in a large US city. Several members of the senior leadership team of a local megachurch met with me for several hours one evening. At the conclusion of our time together, they told me, "We believe the way you are proposing to make disciples will result in more and better fruit than the approaches we are currently using, but we simply cannot pursue that path."

I asked them why. They responded that they had just taken out a loan for more than $60 million to expand their building and could not afford to change their approach on the chance it might result in a decrease in giving. On one hand, I admired their candor. On the other hand, I was aghast that they were willing to place the prosperity of their organization before the Kingdom of God.

There are two very large and widely known Christian ministries that have made it clear for decades that they wanted nothing to do with church planting, *because doing that work might put them in competition with churches, which were their main source of income.* They were unwilling to risk alienating the hand that fed them. I would feel far better about their decision if it were based on a clear word from the Lord, but they never claimed that. In the past decade, one of these two organizations has become convinced of the error of its previous stance and has pivoted toward aggressively pursuing church planting. The other remains unchanged in its approach. One is willing to risk its financial status for the sake of the Kingdom; the other is not.

Another practical issue in corporate settings arises when there is a joint agreement on principles from Scripture but differing interpretations as to how those principles apply to a specific situation. This happens frequently in settings where there is a strong emphasis on knowing Scripture but a relative neglect of listening to the Holy Spirit. This leads to gridlock, compromise, or division.

On the other hand, members of communities that emphasize the Holy Spirit but are not immersed in Scripture or skilled in its interpretation and application often believe they are hearing things from God that are mutually exclusive. This too leads to paralysis or division.

These situations become even more complicated, as noted in the previous chapter, when these communities include individuals who are not believers or who are not walking in the Spirit, thereby making real spiritual unity impossible. We can be of one mind only if we all have the mind of Christ.

Do not misunderstand me. When I speak of unity, I am not simply talking about everyone getting along. That would be like defining peace as an absence of hostility. That is a weak and partial description at best. Unity in the body of Christ will of necessity include laboring collaboratively for Kingdom advance. It means active cooperation toward making God's reign known to all people groups in all places. It means working in alignment to see His purposes pursued and His will done at every level of society.

For this level of joint effort to occur, we must seek unity not only at an individual level but at various corporate levels as well. For this reason, we need an increase in communications among various streams of Christianity. That may not be feasible or practical at an organizational level with streams that are largely nominally Christian, but we need to make provision for it with individuals of good faith in various organizations and cease creating such hard lines of division within the global body of believers. This was the idea behind the creation of the Lausanne Movement back in the 1970s, with its slogan of "the whole church taking the whole gospel to the whole world." There have been other efforts at accomplishing this unity as well, both before and since.

From a practical perspective, this is easier said than done. The following diagram represents what I have found to be a helpful way to think about this issue. The ministry aspects closer to the center of the diagram are ones in which it is helpful to be more cautious and discriminating in establishing partnerships. At the outermost ring there can even be solidarity on some issues with those who are overtly non-Christian. Sometimes the relationships that begin by focusing on an outer ring can develop into more intimate and trusting relationships later. Following this approach can often move relationships and demonstrations of unity far beyond where they might otherwise go.

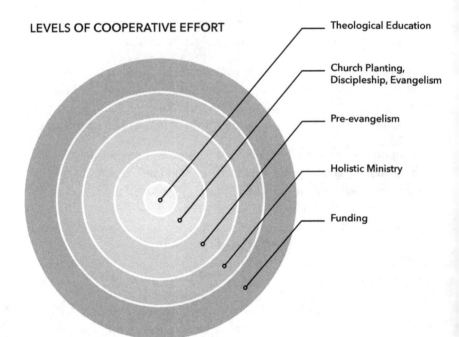

LEVELS OF COOPERATIVE EFFORT

Theological Education

Church Planting,
Discipleship, Evangelism

Pre-evangelism

Holistic Ministry

Funding

PRAYER

Lord Jesus, You came and died so that we could be one as You and the Father are one. This seems impossible. Yet You hold me responsible to pursue unity in Your family. Help me. Help me to love Your children because they are born of You. Help me to consider others more important than myself. Help me to value the different way You have made each one of us. Help me to recognize that I need them. Help me to give up my preferences so they can be built up. Help quiet the voice in my mind that is so quick to criticize others. Show me how I can pursue peace and unity.

QUESTIONS

Read the following questions, then pray and ask God what He wants you to learn and do. Listen quietly.

Review your journal. Are there any past commitments you have not completed? If needed, schedule revised completion dates.

1. How aware am I of the corporate aspects of following the Lord? How can I improve the level of mutuality and unity in my relationships within the body of Christ?

2. What am I doing to pursue unity in the body of Christ? What do I need to do? Are there steps I need to take, personally or as an organization leader?

3. Are there things I am doing or saying that are sowing disunity or discord in the body of Christ?

4. What specific actions does God want me to take in response to this chapter? (Note them in your journal and schedule them in your calendar.)

5. With whom (at least one name) does God want me to share what I have learned?

Ask the Lord to enable you to follow through on these commitments and to prepare the hearts of those with whom you intend to share insights.

11 God Is Our Model for Communication

God's communication is personal, impactful, and authoritative; we need to respond appropriately, and model an appropriate response for others.

Teach me, O Lord, the way of Your statutes,
And I shall observe it to the end.
Give me understanding, that I may observe Your law
And keep it with all my heart.
Make me walk in the path of Your commandments,
For I delight in it.

—PSALM 119:33–35

When God speaks, He means what He says, He does what He says, and He expects us to do what He says. We must learn to treat communication from God differently than the other communications that flood our lives. We live in an age overflowing with messaging—most of which is irrelevant, meaningless, or false. By necessity, we have learned to filter and disregard most of the communication directed at us. We cannot do the same with God.

God is a strategic communicator, and His word is purposeful and powerful. In ISAIAH 55:10-11, the Lord says, "For as the rain and the snow come down from heaven, and do not return there without watering the earth and making it bear and sprout, and furnishing seed to the sower and bread to the eater; So will My word be which goes forth from My mouth; it will not return to Me empty, without accomplishing what I desire, and without succeeding in the matter for which I sent it." In the end, we will submit to Him and conform to His will. The only question is whether we will do so willingly or under compulsion. Will we do so as loved children or as vanquished enemies?

New communication technologies have introduced new patterns of filtering and processing information. Unfortunately, we often apply these same filters to messages from God. These patterns may be perfectly appropriate when applied to messages from other people, but they are decidedly inappropriate when applied to God's communications to us. His messages to us are personal, authoritative, actionable, and important. They demand our full attention and response.

Over the last five hundred years, communication technologies have evolved in amazing fashion, from Gutenberg's printing press to the telegraph, radio, television, and Internet. This evolution has had great impact on our perceptions and practices of communicating. Unquestionably, modern communication technologies have been used to accomplish wonderful things on behalf of the Kingdom of God. However, I also believe that they have had some negative consequences.

Before the printing press, most communications were personal—directed to a particular individual or group. When Paul wrote a letter to Timothy, Timothy did not have to ask, "Does this apply to me?" Of course it applied to him; it had been written specifically for him. With the advent of the printing press, communications became significantly decontextualized. The printing press resulted in a whole new class of writing, more generic and principle-based and less personal. It became necessary for readers to ask themselves, "Does this apply to me? Is this actionable or relevant to my life?" So readers started to filter communications for personal relevance, disregarding those that did not seem to apply to them.

The invention of the telegraph restored the personal nature of communication, as telegrams were usually sent to a specific individual. But it created a new filter, the filter of recency. The information transmitted was of immediate urgency, but not of long-lasting value. New facts pushed other facts out of consciousness quickly. Daily newspapers furthered the trend. Hence the saying, "Yesterday's newspaper is good only to wrap fish." Nonrecent news is not news and should be ignored, according to this attitude.

With radio and then television, people began to assess the value of communication based largely on its entertainment value. This tendency has penetrated the realms of religion and politics, creating a culture in which teaching and entertainment are inseparable.

Radio and TV also shortened people's attention spans. Advertising contributed to this impact, presenting information in neatly packaged thirty-second formats. Storytelling accompanied by images and music became essential. Reasoned arguments and thoughtful analysis were put aside unless they could be packaged in an entertaining one-hour program. The result has been mental passivity and lazy thinking. We have added another filter, often asking, "Is this interesting or amusing to me?" If not, we simply ignore it.

The Internet has exacerbated this tendency, causing people to constantly filter, skim, and summarize in order to deal with data overload. We are swamped by data, often packaged in emotion-laden ways, without the time or information needed to analyze or evaluate.

Twitter has further amplified cultural patterns of brevity, leading to additional degradation of attention spans and prevalence of sound-bite culture. Facebook created greater exacerbation of image-consciousness. Image is valued over content, reputation over character, impression over reality. Communications using that application became about image management.

The profusion of data forces people to filter what they consume. By sheer necessity, we are forced to quickly disregard most of the information that comes at us. We filter it for applicability (Does this apply to me and my situation?), for recency (Is this today's news?), for entertainment value (Do I enjoy this?), for actionability (Is there something for me to do about it?), and for authority (Do I really believe this guy?).

For example, I recently received a recorded message on my cell phone, saying (in a slightly foreign accent): "This is the Social Security Administration. Please contact us immediately before we start legal proceedings." I don't know what the recording said after that, because I hung up, deleted the message, and blocked the number. Why? Because within a few seconds I decided that this was not really the Social Security Administration (real government offices will usually write letters, to preserve a paper trail), and I know lots of people are "phishing" for my personal account information. Twenty years ago I would not have done that.

I would have listened to the whole message. But the proliferation of people trying to sell me something, steal my information, or get me to look at their Twitter feed has forced me to quickly filter incoming information and disregard most of it.

But as we filter, we naturally tend to pay attention to information that confirms our previously held biases. This tendency leads to multiple, sharply defined audiences, each of which exists in a self-reinforcing echo chamber. This has, in turn, resulted in massive fragmentation rather than the previously described unifying function of communications.

The upshot is that we receive more and more information and listen (in the biblical sense of "hear and obey") to less and less. News has transitioned from being functional and actionable to a collection of decontextualized facts. The ratio of information to action has been steadily declining. (Ask yourself how much of TV news is designed to entertain and how little of it has a direct, practical impact on your life.)

These trends are reaching their logical conclusion with big data and artificial intelligence. With these, we delegate responsibility for evaluation and decision making to a computer algorithm, based on predetermined general principles. The impact on thinking patterns, analytical ability, ethics, and other areas of life will be profound. Not that I oppose big data or artificial intelligence; they offer great potential benefits. But we must pay attention to what we can lose along the way.

We are creating a world in which we place our decision-making confidence in data and statistics. Even assuming that the data are accurate and appropriate, and assuming that we interpret the data correctly, a bigger problem remains, for we live in an upside-down Kingdom where the "smart" decision is frequently not the right decision. Think of Joshua marching around Jericho with trumpets blaring (JOSHUA 6), or Gideon sending away the majority of his soldiers (JUDGES 7). Making data-driven decisions could teach us to trust our data rather than God. With so many decisions being premade based on the data, we will not feel our need for God so keenly and will be tempted to listen to God less. Will we trust our software more and listen to God less? Will we begin to outsource or predetermine too many of our decisions?

I am not discounting the value of data or research. God can use research to guide us. In the 1990s, I advised a number of leaders of the Chinese house-church movement in order to help them develop a missions strategy.

Senior leaders in the movement were dismissive of missions research. They would point out that pride drove David to take a census (2 SAMUEL 24:1–25; 1 CHRONICLES 21:1–30). I would respond by pointing out occasions when God approved of censuses (EXODUS 30:11–16; NUMBERS 1:1–46; 4:1–49; 26:1–65; 2 CHRONICLES 2:17–18; 25:5; NEHEMIAH 7:1–68). Then I would argue that the most important function of missions research is to discover where work is *not* happening.

My goal was to get the Chinese leaders to learn about the many unreached people groups in China. Their traditional approach to mission strategy was to seek God's leading, then go where God told them they should go. But there was a problem. They were unaware of the very existence of most of these unreached people groups. It is difficult to go to a place you don't know exists. Once they became aware of these unreached groups, they began to sense God's call to go to them. The data helped them hear God more fully.

The question is not whether we should make decisions based on what we hear from God. Of course we should. But God communicates through many means, including research and intelligent planning. Just as He gives greater knowledge to those who study His Word diligently, He communicates wisdom to those who devote both prayer and careful research to their decisions. Planning is not a bad thing. The question is whether we will plan our trust or trust our plan. We trust in God, not in our planning.

We live in a time that drives us to quickly filter out and disregard most of the communications directed at us. When I go through my mail, I toss most of it in the trash without opening it, based on a quick perusal of the outside of the envelope. I do the same with my email, deleting most of it based on a scan of the sender and subject line. I just don't have time to read it all. That is good, even necessary. But I must fight against the tendency to treat God's communications in the same way. When God speaks—whether in the Bible or through the personal promptings of His Spirit—I need to turn off the filters and carefully attend to all He says. I need to slow down, stop multitasking, and give Him my undivided focus.

In discipleship, we need to remediate the cultural patterns of filtering incoming information. We must restore ways of thinking and communicating that prepare us to hear from God as He speaks to us in personal, timely, authoritative, and impactful ways. We can do that by establishing patterns of interacting with Scripture, with one another, and in prayer that highlight these aspects of God's communications. The remainder of this book contains suggestions regarding small groups, personal discipleship, and personal devotional habits to help us accomplish that goal.

But when evangelizing, we need to communicate in a way that communicates effectively in the culture that exists. *We need to accommodate in evangelism and remediate in disciple making.* We need to evangelize in a way that is understandable to the people we are talking to—suited to their age group and culture. We cannot communicate to people in ways they are not able or willing to receive. The underlying message does not change, but the means of communicating it must be constantly adapted to the contemporary culture. This is what the Incarnation was all about.

Acts 17 provides an example, as Paul preaches two different evangelistic sermons. The first (ACTS 17:1–4) is addressed to Jews in Thessalonica. In this message he argues that Jesus fulfills the Old Testament promises concerning the Messiah. In his second gospel message (ACTS 17:22–32), Paul is speaking to a gathering of Greek philosophers. There he does not mention the Messiah or the Old Testament. Instead, he begins by talking about an altar he had observed in Athens—an altar to an unknown God. Then he quotes a Greek poet to argue that there is one God, creator of all, on whom we all depend. He concludes with the coming judgment before Jesus, who rose from the dead.

Paul gives two different gospel messages because he is speaking to two different audiences. He adapts his message to fit the culture in which he is communicating. In presenting the gospel, we must do the same. Essentially, we must communicate the gospel in the style of the culture.

However, once people have entered the Kingdom as disciples, we need to remediate them. We need to train them to respond to God's communications, not as the culture dictates but in the style in which God chooses to communicate. We need to train them in new patterns of listening so that they can receive God's communications in the way He intends: as personal, authoritative, and calling for a response of obedient action. In the following chapters we will talk about how to do that—how to train and disciple in a way that is designed to encourage people to learn, do, and share God's Word.

Because people are used to filtering and ignoring the bulk of communications directed at them, it is almost impossible to disciple someone who has not acknowledged the Lordship of Christ. We teach them something from God's Word, and they pick and choose what they will apply. This is not biblical discipleship.

They need to have the connection restored between information and action. They need to learn to do what God says. They need to understand the personal and relational and authoritative nature of God's communications. They need to stop thinking of their own communications as a way to manage their personal image and focus, and instead think about how they can bring honor and glory to God. None of this can happen without a prior decision that Jesus is Lord and deserves our obedience.

John Dewey, the famous educator, said, "The content of a lesson is the least important thing about learning." In other words, how one learns is important. Technology impacts ideology and philosophy and behavior. We will learn more about tools to help us make these essential adaptations in later chapters.

PRAYER

Lord, you deserve my immediate, complete, and wholehearted obedience. Your Word is my command. Help me to live that way. I am so used to filtering, evaluating, ignoring, and dismissing incoming communications. Help me to never do that with You. Give me wisdom to understand the culture I live in. Show me how to communicate Your gospel in a way that is true, understandable, and persuasive. Then, help me to train disciples who treat Your Word as they ought.

QUESTIONS

Read the following questions, then pray and ask God what He wants you to learn and do. Listen quietly.

Review your journal. Are there any past commitments you have not completed? If needed, schedule revised completion dates.

1. How do I respond to God's communication—whether written Scripture or personal promptings? Do I filter, evaluate, and choose what to apply, or do I obey immediately, completely, and wholeheartedly?

2. Do I help other followers of Jesus remediate their culturally learned patterns of filtering communications from God?

3. Do I accommodate people's preferred communication patterns in evangelism?

4. How can I improve in those two areas?

5. What specific actions does God want me to take in response to this chapter? (Note them in your journal and schedule them in your calendar.)

6. With whom (at least one name) does God want me to share what I have learned?

Ask the Lord to enable you to follow through on these commitments and to prepare the hearts of those with whom you intend to share insights.

PART

3

PRACTICAL CONCEPTS AND TOOLS TO GROW IN THEOPRAXY

12 Christ Is Both Savior and Lord

God's call to salvation is a call to follow Him regardless of the cost and to be transformed and enabled by the power of the Holy Spirit.

Now large crowds were going along with Him; and He turned and said to them, "If anyone comes to Me, and does not hate his own father and mother and wife and children and brothers and sisters, yes, and even his own life, he cannot be My disciple. Whoever does not carry his own cross and come after Me cannot be My disciple."

—LUKE 14:25–27

The Great Commission in MATTHEW 28:18–20 has three main parts. The first is a description of the power and authority of Jesus: "All authority has been given to Me in heaven and on earth." Second is our mission or job description: "Go therefore and make disciples of all the nations, baptizing them in the name of the Father and the Son and the Holy Spirit, teaching them to observe all that I commanded you. "The third part is a promise of Jesus' presence: "Lo, I am with you always, even to the end of the age."

We love the first and last parts. We love to hear about Jesus' power, Jesus' authority, and the promise that Jesus is with us. The middle part—the mission—is less popular. It sounds like a lot of work and responsibility. But we cannot experience the first and last parts—we will *never* experience the power and presence of Jesus—unless we are doing the second part, the job Jesus gave us.

William Carey, the father of the modern missionary movement, said that the promise of the Great Commission is coextensive with the command. In other words, if Jesus' promise was to all His followers, then His command was as well. Today, many Christians picture the Christian life as a life of quiet communion with Jesus. They look to the story of Mary and Martha (LUKE 10:38–42) to learn how to draw near to Jesus. They seek to experience intimacy with Jesus by sitting at Jesus' feet and listening to His teaching.

This is true, but incomplete. It is true that service cannot earn our salvation and that we must listen constantly and intently to what the Lord says. But if Jesus says, "Go! Make disciples!" then to remain sitting is not to listen—not in the biblical sense. Jesus' words are not merely for our entertainment and comfort, but also for our direction and action. This is how we show our love for Him.

In this part of the book, I will present some tools and practices to help us develop patterns that support a life of Theopraxy. Some people complain that such patterns, habits, or disciplines are deadening and lifeless, and that they interfere with a living and vital relationship with God and others. That objection is illogical, and it has not been my experience. Rather, these patterns or disciplines lay a foundation upon which God builds what He chooses for our lives. As we learn His Word, form habits of obedience, learn to seek Him in prayer, and share what we learn with others, we are preparing ourselves to hear His voice and do His work.

Think of it like eating with silverware and at established mealtimes. Is food boring and bland because we always eat with a knife, fork, and spoon? Are meals rendered meaningless because we use the same implements over and over and over again? Do we lose interest in eating because of the life-draining repetitiveness of the endless cycle of breakfast, lunch, and dinner? Do we stop enjoying food because of these empty habits? No, silverware and mealtimes simply deliver the food to our mouths.

The tools and concepts offered in this section do not take the excitement out of life; rather, they provide a foundation of personal-life discipline that prepares us to hear and respond to God's exciting call. They help us become more intentional in listening to God, pursuing the life He intends for us, knowing Him more deeply, making Him known more effectively, and loving Him more passionately. Let us strive to live our lives in an intentional way, like St. Jerome, so that we might please the One we love.

We must start by correctly understanding the gospel. Often it is preached in a way that maximizes the benefit to us and minimizes the commitment required. It is easy to fall into this pattern. We talk about forgiveness of sins, peace with God, hope of eternal life, and blessing. Those things are all true. But our gospel is not complete unless we also talk about commitment, sacrifice, and putting Jesus ahead of all else.

When Jesus preached, He was very clear about these things. In Jesus' view, the Kingdom of Heaven demands first priority:

> The kingdom of heaven is like a treasure hidden in the field, which a man found and hid again; and from joy over it he goes and sells all that he has and buys that field.
>
> Again, the kingdom of heaven is like a merchant seeking fine pearls, and upon finding one pearl of great value, he went and sold all that he had and bought it. (MATTHEW 13:44–46)

LUKE 14:25–35 gives us a remarkable example of Jesus' thinking. Jesus had attracted a large crowd of followers as He taught, healed, and performed other miracles. Jesus then turned to them and said something startling, as if He were trying to drive the crowd away:

> If anyone comes to Me, and does not hate his own father and mother and wife and children and brothers and sisters, yes, and even his own life, he cannot be My disciple. Whoever does not carry his own cross and come after Me cannot be My disciple. (LUKE 14:26–27)

Jesus is telling them, in essence, "Before you decide to follow me, carefully consider the cost." Following Him, He told His listeners, means treating Him as far more important than their most intimate human relationships, including parents, husbands, wives, and children. It means being ready to die for Him every day, or to give up all their earthly possessions at any time (14:33). Otherwise, Jesus suggested, they were absolutely worthless as His followers—not even good enough for the manure pile (14:35).

Wow! That seems like a terrible way to recruit followers. But Jesus is looking for a particular kind of follower—those who recognize Him as the most important thing in the universe. Here, Jesus was testing the motives of those who were following Him. Were they seeking entertainment? Education? Healing? A free meal? Or, because of what He had been saying and doing, had they recognized who He was: the Creator and Lord of everything? If the latter motive was present, then His demands were completely reasonable, even obvious.

Christians today frequently distort the task of evangelism. We say the good news of the gospel is that we can have our needs met and be blessed. That is true, but it is a secondary benefit. The real good news is that we can know, serve, and have an intimate relationship with the indescribable Lord of all creation—the good, perfect, kind, and loving God.

Because we often preach a low-cost gospel, many who come to God think that anything they do or give up for God is noteworthy or deserves special praise or credit. They evaluate their lives based on their own happiness or comfort. They completely miss the point of discipleship. For a true disciple, every aspect of life centers on the opportunity to know Him and make Him known—to honor, glorify, please, serve, and delight in Him.

A common approach is to invite people "to make a decision for Christ" as quickly as possible, and then afterwards, gently and gradually, to reveal the implications of that decision over time. We introduce the cost of discipleship slowly so as not to scare people off. Eventually, as new believers come to appreciate the privilege of knowing Christ, we tell them the rest of the story.

Sometimes that works, but in many cases the new believers either end up as consumer-oriented Christians or leave the church because they feel as if they've been subjected to "bait and switch" sales tactics. As a consequence, our churches are full of consumer Christians, for whom personal preference—not God's Kingdom—is the deciding value. Either they have never really given their lives to the Lord or they have chosen to remain in an immature state of selfishness and laziness.

As a result, our churches may be full, but they are full of lukewarm, uncommitted believers. This damages both our churches and how the world views us. It also encourages a tendency, even in those who seek to grow, to do so in their own strength rather than by the empowerment of the Holy Spirit—because gradual changes and improvement seem to be within the grasp of human effort.

I might graph this approach in the following way:

This approach is characterized by a low barrier of entry and then a long, gradual pattern of growth. The benefits of being a Christian for this life and the next are emphasized; the cost in terms of personal sacrifice and commitment is downplayed, at least initially.

In contrast, Jesus' approach in LUKE 14 looks like this:

Jesus presented a high, humanly impossible barrier of entry followed by a long, gradual pattern of growth thereafter. He explained the high-entry barrier by focusing on the unrestricted commitment required. He literally sought to drive away the uncommitted. His "church" was relatively empty (of the thousands He had preached to, only 120 were waiting in the upper room in ACTS 1:15), but those remaining few were willing to pay the price.

When the high-entry barrier is clear, there is no question from the very beginning about the source of the power to enter the Kingdom of God or to live as a follower of Jesus. No one could, in their own strength, make the required level of sacrifice. On the contrary, Kingdom life is possible only through the enablement of the Holy Spirit.

Moreover, there is clarity, from the outset, that everything in one's life must be centered on and surrendered to the King and His Kingdom. The emphasis is on responding to the Lord in gratitude, love, and sacrifice for all His kindness, grace, and greatness. No one has to be convinced later that certain additional aspects of their life should be submitted to God. They made that decision at the beginning. They have already decided that whenever they understand God's will, they will obey it by the power of the Holy Spirit.

The difference between these two patterns is described in PSALM 32:8–9:

> I will instruct you and teach you in the way which you should go;
> I will counsel you with My eye upon you.
> Do not be as the horse or as the mule which have no understanding,
> Whose trappings include bit and bridle to hold them in check,
> *Otherwise* they will not come near to you.

The picture of God guiding with His eyes is akin to the master of a well-trained dog—one so attuned to its master's will that a mere glance or gesture is enough to send the dog into action. That is in contrast to a horse or mule, which is not well-trained and responds only to force. People who have not acknowledged the absoluteness of God's authority in their lives are like the untrained mule. They must be forced or convinced to comply. They require a carrot-and-stick approach to guidance. A person who recognizes the Lord's absolute jurisdiction over all of life is simply waiting for direction, attentive to the slightest indication from the Master.

Another contrast between LUKE 14 and our common pattern is illustrated by the diagrams below. Both represent time lines moving from left to right. The cross signifies the point at which a person identifies himself or herself with Christ. The point where the two lines merge into one is the moment when the person recognizes Christ's authority and rule over all of life.

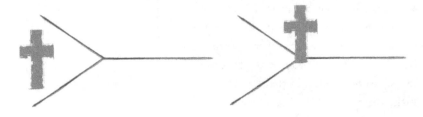

In the diagram on the left, the person must be convinced of any changes or sacrifices the Lord requires. In the diagram on the right, the believer has already decided to follow wherever the Lord leads. The practical consequences are profound and are constantly revealed in behavior and attitude. This is the main reason the world is perpetually accusing the church of hypocrisy—because it's true.

In recent decades, there has been a debate within evangelical circles regarding "Lordship salvation." The question is whether it is possible for a person to be saved without first making a decision to follow Jesus as Lord, or boss. I am not trying to resolve that debate here. That is not the question we are asking in this book. Participants in the "Lordship salvation" debate are asking, in essence, "What's the least someone can do and still be saved?" or "Is it enough if they believe in Jesus' divinity, death, and resurrection, without committing to follow Him?" To me, that seems to be the wrong question. We should not be asking, "What's the least we can do?" but "How can I do the most? How can I best serve Jesus? How can I be a disciple, and make disciples, of the sort Jesus wants?"

It is very clear from Scripture that Jesus' goal for us is not to do the least we can and still make it to heaven. He wants to revolutionize our lives. In fact, He died to change how and why we live: "He died for all, so that they who live might no longer live for themselves, but for Him who died and rose again on their behalf" (2 CORINTHIANS 5:15). And as we make disciples, our goal is to guide them into deeply transformed, obedient lives: "Make disciples of all the nations, . . . teaching them to observe [or obey] all that I commanded you" (MATTHEW 28:19–20).

One practical difference between high-entry barrier and low-entry barrier patterns is manifested in how we follow up with new believers. In the low-barrier approach, new believers are expected to sit back and learn for an extended period of time. We assume that they need to receive teaching for a while before they can be active ambassadors for the Kingdom. The focus is on taking in spiritual knowledge through reading the Bible, prayer, and attending church. They are conditioned to a pattern of passivity and consumption.

In the high-barrier paradigm, follow-up is very different. The immediate focus is on equipping new believers to become active propagators of their faith. They are promptly challenged to become evangelists and church planters. They may be asked to list one hundred people they know and then select five of these people with whom they will immediately share their decision to follow Jesus. They are trained to share the gospel and a simple testimony and then, perhaps after some role-playing practice, to go out to talk with the five people they have selected. If any of those five come to faith, the same follow-up pattern is applied with them. All this can happen *on the first day* a new believer makes a commitment to following Christ! Follow-up and evaluation of their progress usually happen within forty-eight hours in this paradigm.

We are so accustomed to the low-barrier paradigm that this sort of immediate action seems impossible. Yet that is exactly what we see in New Testament examples such as the Gerasene demoniac (MARK 5:19–20),

Levi the tax collector (LUKE 5:27–30), and the Samaritan woman at the well (JOHN 4:28–30).

The pattern established by the high-barrier approach is that whatever the Lord reveals to a believer should be immediately applied and shared with others. This pattern is imprinted from the moment people enter the Kingdom and characterizes their life thereafter. They learn to live like a well-trained dog rather than an untrained mule. They recognize that they, as ambassadors for the Kingdom, will have the privilege of being a conduit of God's grace and love for people for the rest of their lives. Life is lived expectantly, as they never know what new challenge or adventure lies around the next bend. Confidence in the Lord is built up daily, as they listen for and respond to His daily direction and experience His sufficiency for them continually in new ways.

PRAYER

Lord, I want to be like the well-trained dog eagerly watching for Your glance to send me dashing off in tail-wagging obedience. But I can sometimes be more like a mule. Change my heart. You deserve my obedience, and I gain nothing by delaying or resisting. The path of obedience is the path of true blessing. Stubbornness and reluctance will not bring joy nor fruitfulness nor glory to You. I am sorry. By Your Spirit, give me ears to listen and a heart to obey.

QUESTIONS

Read the following questions, then pray and ask God what He wants you to learn and do. Listen quietly.

Review your journal. Are there any past commitments you have not completed? If needed, schedule revised completion dates.

1. Do I hear from God and then decide whether or not to obey, or has my commitment to obedience already been resolved in my mind and heart? How can I promote the latter approach in my life and the lives of other believers I know?

2. Am I proclaiming a "low-entry barrier" gospel or a Luke 14 "high-entry barrier" gospel? How should I adjust my proclamation to better imitate Jesus?

3. When I follow up with new believers, am I training them to obey and share immediately, or am I encouraging them to learn passively?

4. What specific actions does God want me to take in response to this chapter? (Note them in your journal and schedule them in your calendar.)

5. With whom (at least one name) does God want me to share what I have learned?

Ask the Lord to enable you to follow through on these commitments and to prepare the hearts of those with whom you intend to share insights.

13 Christ Has Our Exclusive Allegiance

The Lord should not be merely the greatest of competing aspects of our lives, but rather the defining theme of every aspect of our lives.

For from Him and through Him and to Him are all things.
To Him be the glory forever. Amen.

—ROMANS 11:36

The number *one* is meaningful. It implies uniqueness, solidarity, and supremacy. There is only one true north.

When I was a child, I lived in South Korea. The Koreans are a very competitive people and passionate about sports. Back then, when you watched any sport, you immediately knew which player was the best on each team, because that player wore the number 1. In that context, one meant *best*. In reference to God, one means *only*. It is exclusive.

When the writers of Scripture tell us that God is jealous, as they do many times, they have this sense of exclusiveness in mind. God even says His name is Jealous in EXODUS 34:14. Just as marriage is intended to be exclusive, so we are to belong exclusively to Him. No one else is to be worshiped, trusted, relied on, loved, served, or glorified. God does not share well with others, because there are no others. Nothing can be compared with Him in any sense. God thinks He is worthy of 100 percent of our worship, and He is not willing to share.

> I am the Lord, that is My name;
> I will not give My glory to another,
> Nor My praise to graven images. (ISAIAH 42:8)

Relying on God alone pleases Him as much as worshiping Him alone. Whatever we desire, praise, serve, admire, or love that is other than Him is something to repent of. Our thinking is warped or blinded if He is not the sole object of our lives.

In physics, scientists are earnestly seeking a Grand Unified Theory that will tie together all the branches of physics into a consistent and connected whole. God has already revealed Himself as the Grand Unified Reality. In COLOSSIANS 1:15–20, Jesus is presented as the source, maintainer, and redeemer of everything in all creation, both visible and invisible.

> For by Him all things were created, both in the heavens and on earth, visible and invisible, whether thrones or dominions or rulers or authorities—all things have been created through Him and for Him. He is before all things, and in Him all things hold together. (COLOSSIANS 1:16–17)

Note what this passage says: All things were created by, through, and for Christ. He is, quite literally, the source and purpose of everything.

In DEUTERONOMY, in the passage that Jews call the *Shema*, God tells His people that He alone is God and commands them to love Him with all their being (DEUTERONOMY 6:4–9). They are told to use physical reminders to keep God at the forefront of their minds—when they are at home or away from home, for themselves and for others, publicly and privately, when rising and when retiring for the night. His worthiness and greatness are to be their constant meditation, the sea they swim in.

In the 1600s, the monk Brother Lawrence spoke of "practicing the presence of God," by which he meant a constant awareness of the Lord's presence and conversation with Him. For me, this constant relationship means seeing all of life from His perspective. Rather than imagining myself sitting across from Him, I visualize sitting in His lap, facing out. I hear His voice bringing to my attention whatever He desires to bring it to.

This exclusive focus on God affects my relations to other people. I view it like a pair of eyeglasses with two lenses. The first lens focuses on those with whom I have ongoing relationships (family, friends, neighbors, coworkers, classmates). The second relates to those who are outside my routine relational patterns.

With this first lens, God focuses me on my close relationships. God has positioned each of us in our own families, friendships, and social circles for a reason. He wants to use us to glorify Him to them. Our long-term interactions with these people are to be stewarded every bit as much as our money, time, energy, or any other resource. Many of these people may not now seem open to God. But because God has put them close to me, my job with them is to persist in prayer, in demonstrating God's love to them, and in sharing the truth about God. With them, I can never give up.

For those outside my normal network, I rely heavily on God's guidance as to where and when to focus. This lens is tinted to highlight the last, the least, and the lost. Those are, after all, God's favorites. Scripture is full of evidence of God's special concern for the despised, forsaken, downtrodden, forgotten, disadvantaged, and powerless. But God is often unpredictable, so I need to be sensitive to His prompting to interact with anyone.

In this arena, I generally find that the Lord directs me toward those in whom He is already working to draw them toward Him. So outside my circle of close relationships, I am listening carefully to God's voice to hear how He will direct me to help the disadvantaged and show me those in whom He is already working.

To increase people's sensitivity to their stewardship of their relationships, I ask believers whom I am discipling to make a list of one hundred people they know. They then divide them into three categories: Christian, non-Christian, and unknown. Their next steps will vary, depending on which category each person falls into. For unknowns, the first task is to discover where they are spiritually; for non-Christians, to evangelize; for Christians, to train and encourage.

Many people think about spirituality in terms of two distinct groups. To them, every individual is either in the Kingdom of God or outside it. The first diagram illustrates this bounded-set thinking; the second depicts centered-set thinking.

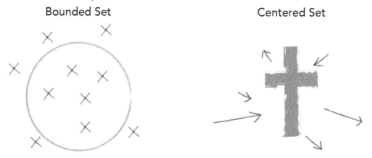

Bounded Set   Centered Set

There is nothing wrong with bounded-set thinking. It is helpful and relevant. It is indeed true that every person is either in or outside the Kingdom of God. Bounded-set thinking helps to emphasize the priority of making sure that people enter the Kingdom. This value is illustrated by Jesus' story of the shepherd who leaves the ninety-nine sheep to seek the one lost sheep (LUKE 15:4–7).

Nonetheless, centered-set thinking is a helpful supplement. In the diagram of the centered set, the allegiance of a particular person is denoted by the direction of the arrow. Arrows pointing toward the cross signify people who have committed their lives to Jesus. But the arrows vary in length, and the length of the arrow indicates the degree of their passion. Some people are radically pursuing a different goal in life, whereas others are doing so only mildly. Some who follow Christ do so passionately, others only tepidly.

God's desire (and hopefully ours as well) is to redirect all the arrows so they point toward the cross. God does not delight in the death of any person (EZEKIEL 18:23, 32; 33:11). He is not wishing that any should perish (2 PETER 3:9), and He desires that all may come to faith (1 TIMOTHY 2:3–4). These truths should guide our interactions with everyone who does not yet know God.

God also wants to lengthen the arrows that already point toward the cross. Those who are already committed to Christ need to increase the level of their commitment. This is true for all of us. None of us love God with all our heart, mind, soul, and strength, twenty-four hours per day, 365 days per year. Hopefully we are progressing toward that goal, though for many believers the trend is in the opposite direction.

This means that whenever we interact with people who already love and serve the Lord, our intention should be to increase their love for Him. We should think carefully and conscientiously about how best to do this. "Consider how to stimulate one another to love and good deeds" (HEBREWS 10:24). We all need that sort of encouragement from others, whether those others are ahead of us or behind us in their own commitment.

With regard to those who don't know the Lord, centered-set thinking is still helpful. It helps us understand that the arrow can be gradually turned, step by step, until it points toward the cross, and that different individuals have different levels of resistance or responsiveness to God.

The following chart helps to portray this principle. The attitude, is depicted by the y-axis, with knowledge as the x-axis. So, for sake of illustration, Satan would be far to the right (high knowledge) and very low (bad attitude, extremely opposed to God). Normally, an unbeliever starts out with very little knowledge and a negative attitude or view of God. But the multiple contacts illustrated in the chart produce gradual change in knowledge and attitude, moving the person toward the cross. In centered-set thinking, this would be shown by a gradual rotation of the arrow to point toward the cross, along with increasing intensity (length).

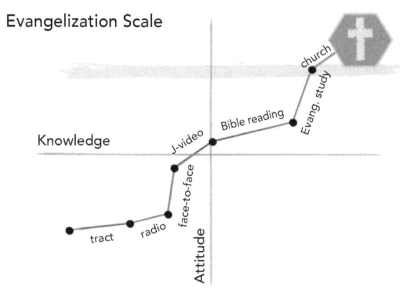

Evangelization Scale

For individuals with whom you have repeated contact, this is a helpful way to visualize the process of drawing them to the Lord. Typically, people have numerous encounters with Christians, which move them closer and closer, before they finally decide to follow Christ.

For individuals with whom you do not have repeated contact, this serves as a reminder to be alert for people who are nearing a point of submission to the Lord and for opportunities to nudge them closer to that point. It also reduces the sense of pressure to seek to bring every person to that position in every interaction. It highlights that your interaction with them is likely one in a series of events that God will use to draw them to Himself.

Having God's perspective goes far beyond personal interactions with people, however. It involves all of life. As the Creator, God is concerned for and engaged with all that exists. He is redeeming not only humans but all creation (ROMANS 8:18–23). He can guide us in stewarding and making proper, creative use of creation. He also reveals Himself in the patterns of nature. If we listen to God, we can learn about Him from all things He created and can make contributions to every branch of learning.

We have the privilege of living inquisitive lives, constantly posing questions about what we see. I frequently ask the Lord what I can learn from one thing or another. Some of these questions have led to specific insights and breakthroughs in my thinking. I have inquired about the Coca-Cola Company, the U.S. Marine Corps, bicycles, farming, photography, waves, rappelling, kayaks, musical instruments, and scuba diving. I ask questions about elephants, rabbits, horses, mules, lizards, frogs, starfish, octopuses, dolphins, geese, ducks, and other animals. I ask about communication technologies, business practices, economics, government, transportation, educational principles, and much more.

Many of the disciple making, church planting, and missiological insights I have gleaned over the years have come from these disparate sources rather than from seminary classes or theological books. There is no limit to God's knowledge about every topic. Why not ask Him?

We can also contribute to all fields of learning from the insights God gives us. George Washington Carver had this habit of asking God about things. He worked in Alabama, near where I currently live. His life and legacy as a follower of Christ, a scientist, and an educator are remarkable. While president of the Tuskegee Institute, he made a world-changing discovery in a most unlikely setting. In his book *Sanctuary of the Soul: Journey into Meditative Prayer*, Richard Foster tells the story:

> George Washington Carver was one of our great scientists, and he often prayed, addressing God as "Mr. Creator." One night he walked out into the woods and prayed, "Mr. Creator, why did you make the universe?" He listened, and this is what he heard: "Little man, that question is too big for you. Try another!" The next night he walked into the woods and prayed, "Mr. Creator, why did you make man [meaning, the human race]?" He listened and he heard this: "Little man, that question is still too big for you. Try another!" The third night he went into the woods and prayed, "Mr. Creator, why did you make the peanut?" This is what he heard: "Little man, that question is just your size. You listen and I will teach you."

The rest is history, as Carver developed hundreds of uses for the peanut and changed the economy of the American South.

No matter what field of work you are engaged in, God knows far more about it than you or anyone else ever will. He can give you insights if you simply ask Him. As St. Augustine said, "All truth is God's truth."

Recognizing God's concern for and involvement with all aspects of life is part of developing spiritual sensitivity. ZEPHANIAH 1:12 speaks of those who do not discern God's activity in the world as being "stagnant in spirit." This is clearly something that displeases the Lord.

Every person has a worldview—a way of interpreting our world—though many have never reflected consciously on their worldview or evaluated it in any formal way. There are seven main aspects of a worldview:

1. Epistemology: What is true?
2. Metaphysics: What is real?
3. Cosmology: What is the nature and purpose of the universe?
4. Teleology: What is the purpose and destiny of everything?
5. Theology: What is the nature and purpose of God (or gods)?
6. Anthropology: What is the nature and purpose of humankind?
7. Axiology: What is meaningful, valuable, and beautiful?

Obviously, in this book I cannot begin to thoroughly explore the dimensions of worldviews in general or the Christian worldview in particular. But for Christians, God must be the center and source of truth regarding all aspects of our worldview. He alone is the arbiter of truth. He has created and determined what is real. The universe exists for His pleasure and purpose. He is infinitely good and great. He made us and gives us purpose. He alone determines meaning, value, and beauty.

For this reason, knowing and understanding Him to the best of our ability matters greatly. That is the only way to rightly understand the world or anything else that exists. Consequently, Theopraxy—living a life centered on and based in God—is the very essence of a Christian worldview.

If you want to pursue this topic in depth, numerous books and even careers have been devoted to pursuing a thorough understanding of the Christian worldview and its implications. A good place to see a list of people who have studied and written about Christian worldview from a range of perspectives is christianworldview.net. You can then go to other resources to pursue greater detail about their views. I believe Francis Schaeffer's writings offer an excellent starting point. His approach is accessible but not watered down, and he works from a solid set of assumptions.

HEBREWS 11 stands as an example of a Christian worldview at work. One of the most common questions that skeptics ask Christians is "If God is so good and powerful, why do bad things happen to good people?" HEBREWS 11 answers that question. This chapter expounds on the theme of faith. Initially, it describes the lives of the famous heroes of the Christian faith: Abel, Enoch, Noah, Abraham, Isaac, Jacob, Joseph, Moses, Rahab, Gideon, Barak, Samson, Jephthah, David, Samuel, and the prophets (HEBREWS 11:4–35). These are the famous "winners" of the life of faith, people to whom God granted victory and fame. But the passage goes on to describe others who were not nearly so famous or victorious—at least, not from a worldly point of view:

> Others were tortured, not accepting their release, so that they might obtain a better resurrection; and others experienced mockings and scourgings, yes, also chains and imprisonment. They were stoned, they were sawn in two, they were tempted, they were put to death with the sword; they went about in sheepskins, in goatskins, being destitute, afflicted, ill-treated (men of whom the world was not worthy), wandering in deserts and mountains and caves and holes in the ground. (HEBREWS 11:35B–38)

Who were these people who suffered so? I don't know. I don't recognize those stories. But God knows. And God says about all of them, the famous and the obscure, life's winners and life's losers:

> And all these, having gained approval through their faith, did not receive what was promised, because God had provided something better for us, so that apart from us they would not be made perfect. (HEBREWS 11:39–40)

In verses 32–35A, the "good guys" win after a struggle. But in verses 35B–38, the good guys are defeated and suffer torture and violent death. Why are these individuals cited as models of faith?

Evidently, from a heavenly perspective, the earthly outcome or results of faith have nothing to do with how things turn out for the faithful person. Rather, the identifying characteristic of faithful people is their readiness to trust God absolutely, so as to bring Him glory. Sometimes He is glorified through a dramatic rescue; sometimes He is glorified by the faithful willingness of His people to suffer and die in obscurity for His sake. God is glorified when His people are willing to risk everything and sacrifice anything for the privilege of serving Him. What could possibly demonstrate His worthiness more than that?

As this passage demonstrates, a Christian worldview accounts for suffering by recognizing that this fallen world is not the end of the story and that a life of faith glorifies God no matter what the earthly outcome. In the final analysis, we who trust in Christ will win and receive our eternal reward. The story ends well for those who live lives of faith on earth.

A Christian worldview will be at variance with virtually any competing worldview, because it makes God the only criterion for determining meaning, truth, purpose, value, or destiny. We need to strive for this eternal perspective as we seek to follow Paul's admonition: "Do not be conformed to this world, but be transformed by the renewing of your mind, so that you may prove what the will of God is, that which is good and acceptable and perfect" (ROMANS 12:2).

PRAYER

Lord, renew my mind. Help me to view every aspect of life in the light of You. Help me to see every interaction with others in terms of how You can be more greatly appreciated and acknowledged in their lives. Teach me eternal truths from what I experience in this temporal existence. Show me how to be Your instrument of blessing to others in all I say and do.

QUESTIONS

Read the following questions, then pray and ask God what He wants you to learn and do. Listen quietly.

Review your journal. Are there any past commitments you have not completed? If needed, schedule revised completion dates.

1. Do I see my relationship with God as one aspect of my life or as the defining foundation of every aspect of my life? How can I keep daily constant reminders of His presence and perspective before in front of me?

2. Are there specific aspects of my worldview (epistemology, metaphysics, cosmology, teleology, theology, anthropology, and axiology) that I need to bring more into God-focus?

3. How effectively am I stewarding the ongoing relationships in my life? How can I be more intentional in helping those people who already love God to continue to grow in Him? How can I be more intentional in helping draw those who do not know God into a loving relationship with Him?

4. Do I consistently seek to be a blessing to every person with whom I come in contact? How can I increase my frequency of doing so?

5. Do I have a habit of asking God for spiritual insight from the situations I encounter day by day? How can I develop this habit?

6. Do I regularly ask the Lord for wisdom in matters related to my work and life? How can I develop this habit?

7. What specific actions does God want me to take in response to this chapter? (Note them in your journal and schedule them in your calendar.)

8. With whom (at least one name) does God want me to share what I have learned?

Ask the Lord to enable you to follow through on these commitments and to prepare the hearts of those with whom you intend to share insights.

14 3/3: A Pattern for Faithful Living

The disciple worth reproducing actively grows in and balances learning, doing, and sharing insights with others.

Just as the Father has loved Me, I have also loved you; abide in My love. If you keep My commandments, you will abide in My love; just as I have kept My Father's commandments and abide in His love.

—JOHN 15:9–10

The best way to improve your ability to hear God is to respond immediately and completely when you do recognize Him speaking. God holds us accountable for how we respond to the opportunities and instructions He gives us. His future dealings with us, as well as our future growth and development, are directly related to how we respond now.

God measures value very differently than the world. The earthly economy is based on exchanges. I have something I want (a pastrami sandwich, for example). You have something I want (money). You give me some of your money and, in exchange, I give you my pastrami sandwich. You pay me for what you want. I do not give it away for free.

In contrast, in the heavenly economy, I gain by giving. I profit by what I freely offer. Consider God's view of forgiveness as an example. In both a parable (MATTHEW 18:23–35) and direct exposition (MATTHEW 6:14–15), Jesus taught that God freely forgives us if we freely forgive others. God has given generously to us. We are to pass it on. We are blessed when we freely give. We gain by giving.

This counterintuitive principle recurs frequently in the New Testament. Jesus says in MATTHEW 10:8, "Freely you received, freely give," and in LUKE 12:48, "From everyone who has been given much, much will be required." Paul tells Timothy to pass on what he received (2 TIMOTHY 2:2), and he summarizes Jesus' teaching as "It is more blessed to give than to receive" (ACTS 20:35).

God gives to us. And we are stewards of what He has given, responsible for freely passing it on to others. The main point of the parable of the talents, in MATTHEW 25:14–30, is that God will hold us accountable for how we steward what He has given us.

The heavenly economy is also prominent in the Old Testament. From the beginning of God's dealings with His people, we see that He blesses us so that we can bless others. When God called Abram (before He had changed his name to Abraham), He said:

> Go forth from your country,
> And from your relatives
> And from your father's house,
> To the land which I will show you;
> And I will make you a great nation,
> *And I will bless you,*
> And make your name great;
> And *so you shall be a blessing;*
> And I will bless those who bless you,
> And the one who curses you I will curse.
> And *in you all the families of the earth will be blessed.*
> (GENESIS 12:1–3, emphasis added)

God promises to bless Abraham, but He has a clear purpose: that Abraham will in turn be a blessing to others—in fact, to all the nations of the world. In the divine economy, we receive in order to give. Abraham was blessed to be a blessing.

God tells us that He chose Abraham to be the father of His people because Abraham obeyed Him (GENESIS 22:15–18; 26:2–5). This obedience is at the very heart of the spiritual economy and of accountability to God. It deserves a close examination. Abraham was not perfect. For example, he tried to pass Sarah off as his sister, not once but twice. He did, however, repeatedly demonstrate immediate, radical, costly obedience.

God called Abraham to leave his country, his father's house, and his relatives and go to a place God would show him. He went. He obeyed immediately (Genesis 12:1–4). This was a major risk. Abraham was leaving a safe, populated, familiar area in favor of wandering in the wilderness through a region full of threatening inhabitants.

Genesis 17 presented another test. God changed Abram's name to Abraham and commanded him to circumcise all the males in his household as a sign of the covenant. Apart from the obvious physical discomfort involved, there was also a potential security issue to consider. In Genesis 34:13–31, Abraham's great-grandchildren would wipe out an entire tribe after its males had been circumcised, because they were unable to defend themselves while healing from the procedure. Abraham, however, did not hesitate. We are told twice, for emphasis, that on the very day God told him this, he circumcised himself, his son Ishmael, every male born in his household, and every male bought with his money (Genesis 17:23–27).

The stakes increase in Genesis 21:9–19. Sarah was upset because Ishmael (Abraham's son through Sarah's servant Hagar) was mocking her son Isaac. She demanded Abraham send away both Ishmael and Hagar. Abraham was deeply troubled by the prospect of sending his son away. God instructed him, though, to listen to Sarah's request. Without delay, he rose early the next morning and sent them away.

In Genesis 22:1–14, Abraham's obedience faced its greatest challenge. God asked him to sacrifice his son Isaac as a burnt offering. Isaac was the son of the promise, for whom Abraham had hoped and waited until he was one hundred years old. Without questioning or pausing, Abraham obeyed. He rose early the next morning and set out for the mountain where God instructed him to do this unthinkable deed. Just as he was raising the knife to kill Isaac, God stopped him and provided a substitute sacrifice in the form of a ram.

Abraham was ready and willing to obey God no matter what the cost. Hebrews 11:17–19 tells us his willingness came from his faith that God could and would raise his son from the dead. Two things are certain in this story: Abraham loved and fully trusted God, and God was pleased with him. In fact, God promised that his offspring would be a great multitude, like the number of stars in the sky or the grains of sand on a beach (Genesis 22:15–17).

Why is Abraham's unhesitating obedience so significant to God? From God's perspective, love for God is the most important aspect of a person's life (MATTHEW 22:34–38), and our love is measured by our obedience (JOHN 14:15; 1 JOHN 5:3). In other words, immediate, radical, costly obedience is both the demonstration and the necessary consequence of loving God with all one's heart, mind, soul, and strength. This is the sort of person God befriends. This is why Abraham was chosen as the spiritual parent of God's people.

Abraham is described as the father of our faith, and we are told to emulate him. We too demonstrate our love for God by our immediate, radical, costly obedience. We can expect Him to speak to us. We have the opportunity to love and fully trust Him because of all He has done for us in rescuing us from eternal death and making us His beloved children and coworkers. This is God's primary measure of our love for Him.

But realistically, we often fall short of this sort of immediate, radical, costly obedience. We often hesitate, make excuses, or simply refuse to obey. Nevertheless, our goal, with God's help, is to move forward in the direction of complete obedience.

But how? This does not happen by wishing it were so. One key aid is mutual accountability with our Christian brothers and sisters. We hold each other accountable to do what we know God wants us to do. In this way, we help each other grow in obedience, become better stewards of the blessings God has given us, and more fully experience the blessings that God has for His obedient children.

Accountability is often viewed as something unpleasant, especially in an employment context where it may involve discipline for subpar performance. But in a Christian context, holding one another accountable is one of the most loving things we can do for one another. We do it out of a genuine desire that others may know the Lord more deeply and experience the joy and fulfillment of living the abundant life He intends for us. We want them to hear God more clearly and to experience the joy of fulfilling the destiny for which God designed them. We want them to benefit from the spiritual economy by faithfully obeying what they hear from the Lord and passing on to others what they are learning from Him. The best thing I can do for others is to help them establish the life pattern of learning, doing, and sharing what God says. We do this through mutual accountability.

How can we live in such a way that this becomes our natural and routine course of action? I would propose that we look at our lives like a stool with three legs: *knowing, doing* (obedience), and *sharing with others.* Just as a three-legged stool with very uneven legs is useless, so unbalanced discipleship is useless. Our knowledge needs to be balanced with doing and sharing. Otherwise, our discipleship is incomplete and truncated, even useless from God's perspective.

The church often places great emphasis on Bible knowledge and equates it with maturity. That is unfortunate. Knowledge without obedience is worthless. In fact, it is worse than worthless, because it incurs additional judgment. As Jesus says, the servant "who knew his master's will and did not get ready or act in accord with his will, will receive many lashes, but the one who did not know *it,* and committed deeds worthy of a flogging, will receive but few" (LUKE 12:47–48). Knowing without doing earns additional punishment. As James says, "To one who knows *the* right thing to do and does not do it, to him it is sin" (JAMES 4:17).

The only appropriate measure of maturity is in terms of one's conformity to the image of Christ (EPHESIANS 4:13). It is God's will that we be so conformed (ROMANS 8:29). *We err if we compare ourselves to anything other than God's will for us or if we pursue His will in any way other than by His Spirit.*

Maturity takes time. Time does not, however, guarantee maturity. Many are still spiritual infants even though they have been Christians for many years. Instead of maturity, we should focus on *faithfulness.* That is something even a brand-new Christian can exhibit. A new follower of Christ can be fully faithful to what he or she knows at that point. If we are faithful to God every day, over time God will make us mature. This is a corollary to the spiritual economy. God is a wise investor. He invests in those who are faithful. This is a key lesson from the parable of the talents in MATTHEW 25:14–30.

The most practical way to assess faithfulness is to examine the ratio of the three legs of the stool I described above—knowing, doing, and sharing. Consider the following figure. For simplicity, it represents three people with equal spiritual knowledge. They all know the same amount, but their lives are not equally pleasing to the Lord.

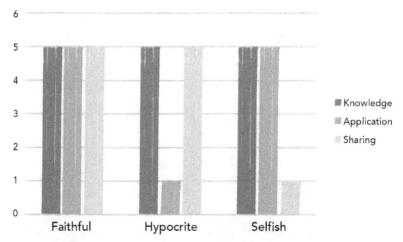

The first person in this graph is faithful. What she knows, she does and shares with others. The second is a hypocrite. He knows what he should do, and he preaches it to others, but he does not put it into practice in his own life. The third is selfish. He is learning and putting knowledge into practice in his own life, but not sharing with others.

Just as a three-legged stool is useless if the legs are not of similar length, a disciple who does not balance these three aspects is not being faithful to God's call. In the physical realm, if we breathed in but never breathed out, we would die within ten minutes. But we do the same thing in the spiritual realm when we constantly take in new knowledge without applying it to our own lives or sharing it with others who can benefit from it.

Together with accountability, there are several practical approaches that you can insert into your daily routine to promote balance and consistency in your spiritual breathing. One of them is what I call the three-thirds (or 3/3). The three thirds are as follows:

1.) Look back   2.) Look up   3.) Look forward

These correspond to the three legs of the stool. The "look up" portion represents the knowledge leg of the stool. The "look back" and "look forward" portions are focused on evaluating and planning the "do" and "share with others" legs. In other words, you look back to evaluate your prior activities in doing and sharing, and you look forward to determine how the Lord is asking you to engage in doing and sharing and to plan how to carry out His direction.

We use this structure in our house church. I also use it in my daily Bible study, in follow-up after training events, and in leadership and mentoring meetings. I spend one-third of the available time looking back to evaluate what has happened since the last meeting, especially our commitments to do or share from the previous session. The second third is focused on looking up to God in search of new insights and impressions from Scripture or from the Holy Spirit. Finally, we look forward and make specific plans to put into practice what we have learned and share it with others. The "look forward" component ensures that we never stop at gaining knowledge, but always do and share what we have learned.

Because the 3/3 format has become an ingrained habit, every time I open my Bible, pray, or interact with someone, I am thinking about whether there is something the Lord wants to teach me (knowledge) and have me do or share. This helps to prevent me from becoming a receiver rather than a giver. It also keeps me from becoming hypocritical and heaping judgment upon myself by learning things and talking about them to others, but never putting them into practice in my own life.

As I explain the 3/3 process, I frequently hear two concerns: (1) that believers will fall into heresy because we are encouraging people without formal theological training to interpret and apply Scripture, and (2) that it is works-based legalism to ask people to make specific goals to do and share, and to hold them accountable to those goals. I will address both of these objections in turn.

The concern regarding heretical theology is so deeply and widely expressed that I want to examine it in some detail. In evaluating this concern, we should first ask whether theologically trained leadership effectively prevents heretical beliefs. In 2018, Lifeway Ministries and Ligonier Ministries published the results of a large-scale study on theological knowledge. You can read more about it at thestateoftheology.com. The site has a link at the bottom where you can go to look at all the data from the study.

Part of the study focused on the beliefs of evangelical Christians—defined as those who strongly agree that the Bible is the highest authority, evangelism is very important, sin can be removed only by Jesus' death, and salvation comes only through trusting Jesus as Savior.

The study found that evangelical Christians hold heretical beliefs regarding at least a dozen major doctrines. For example, fewer than one-quarter believe that Jesus is eternal, recognizing that He was not created. Fewer than one-third believe that the Holy Spirit is a personal being. Just 30 percent believe that the Holy Spirit gives new life only after a person has faith in Christ. Only 41 percent believe that people are not good by nature. Only 40 percent believe that the smallest sin is deserving of eternal punishment. These are not peripheral issues; they are core doctrines. The bottom line is that evangelical Christians in the United States widely hold heretical beliefs on primary aspects of theology.

This is the actual result of a system where theologically trained church leaders are the primary teachers of doctrine. The expectation is that theological training will result in good doctrine being taught from the pulpits, and that this in turn will lead to orthodox beliefs in the pews. The study suggests that this approach has not worked as intended. In fact, it appears that most evangelical Christians have seriously heretical theology. This problem has remained largely undetected until now, mainly because the people in the pews are not called on, in a church setting, to say what they actually believe. It is simply assumed that they understand and believe what they have been taught. That is evidently not the case.

We are treating church members as passive recipients in spiritual matters. They are not trained or expected to be responsible for their own growth and development or to minister to others. For the most part, ministry is viewed as the responsibility of professional ministers. Most Christians are not challenged *and held accountable* to be obedient followers and active propagators of their faith, but are allowed to be mere spiritual consumers.

So it appears that having theologically trained leadership preaching to passive members is not an effective way to avoid heresy. What about lay-led 3/3 groups? Do they also result in deviant theology? If you are involved in a group of new believers using the 3/3 pattern to interpret and apply Scripture, you will likely hear some heretical or questionable things said. You will hear those things because the members are encouraged to speak. They are being taught to interpret and apply Scripture for themselves.

Over time, the accuracy of what they believe and say will improve, as they become familiar with a greater volume of Scripture and gain facility in interpreting and applying it. This happens in concert with the practices introduced in the next chapter, which result in each member reading twenty-five or more chapters weekly. The resulting pattern is similar to the graph below, which represents a time line moving from left to right.

The horizontal line represents accurate teaching or belief. The curved line represents the variance from that accurate understanding.

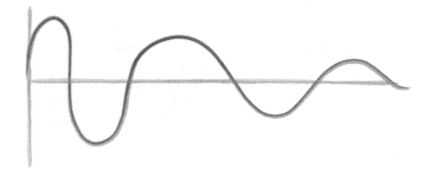

With participative 3/3 groups, we observe improvement, over time, in understanding of and adherence to orthodox Christian truth. We don't see the same sort of improvement over time among people who are sitting in the pews week after week as passive spiritual consumers. We need to question some of our familiar church habits.

When I was serving as a vice president for global strategy with the Southern Baptist International Mission Board, one of the departments under my purview was the Global Research Department (GRD). The GRD did a dozen large-scale, formal studies on movements that used the 3/3 approach together with large Scripture consumption. The settings were unreached people groups who subsequently experienced large church-planting movements that grew quickly. In these settings, no mature believers were available because all the followers of Christ were new in their faith. The concern was that patterns of heresy might develop as a result. So as to reduce bias, these studies were conducted by teams of researchers from various   organizations. They included in-depth interviews of individuals from a wide range of roles and backgrounds and—when possible, in order to get 360-degree evaluations—Christians from neighboring people groups and even non-Christians in the area.

No significant patterns of heresy were found among those dozen movements. The closest thing was among the Kui people of Orissa, India, who had adopted a pattern of delaying baptism until new believers had demonstrated the validity of their conversion over time. This view is not biblical, but it is a tertiary rather than a primary issue. Certainly the timing of baptism is less central than the heresies held by American evangelicals in the study cited above. I am not saying that heresy is impossible when using this approach; but based on these dozen studies, I can safely say that it is not typical or expected.

As a practical example, when I was working in China, about a dozen students at one university came to faith in the fall semester. All of them came from entirely atheistic backgrounds and had no previous contact with Christianity. In the middle of the spring semester, we had a retreat for these young believers. As a fun activity, we took cards from a Bible trivia game and asked the group a total of 700 Bible trivia questions. We allowed them to work together. Collectively, they answered 698 (or 99.7 percent) of the 700 questions correctly.

Having played Bible trivia many times with believers in the United States, I can tell you that this would not be typical even of longtime Christians here. Keep this example in mind when you read the next chapter as well, because this result was due as much to their large daily consumption of Scripture as their thorough examination of Bible passages together. The point is that they were not simply being taught; rather, they were being trained to teach themselves. As a result, they quickly gained a level of Bible knowledge that we would consider very unusual in our American churches and almost unimaginable among such new believers.

This makes sense from the perspective of education theory. The most effective ways to learn include self-discovery, practicing what is learned, teaching others, and repetition. The 3/3 approach includes all of those techniques. The repetition is achieved when one is teaching others and hearing them respond with their own insights and instruction.

Imagine telling someone who has never ridden a bicycle to sit on a couch for twenty-one days and watch the Tour de France. Your student would have the best riders in the world as models to emulate. At the end of the race, imagine taking the person outside and telling him or her to start riding a bicycle. It wouldn't work very well! Why, then, do we expect church members to learn to interpret Scripture by watching their pastor do it? To learn to ride a bicycle, you have to get on the bicycle, crash a few times, and practice a lot. That is how we learn any skill. Similarly, to learn how to interpret and apply Scripture, you have to practice doing it yourself (probably poorly, at first) rather than merely watching others do it.

Learning to ride a bicycle usually entails falling down repeatedly. The same will be true of learning to interpret and apply Scripture. Mistakes will be made. But that is not a sufficient reason to avoid teaching people to do it. They will improve with practice.

Therefore, to build strong disciples, we need to have them in small groups where they learn to discover God's truth for themselves, apply it, and share it with others. Making disciples is an indispensable part of being a disciple, so everyone needs to be engaged in all three legs of the stool (MATTHEW 28:18–20).

The cry of "Legalism!" is the second frequent objection to the 3/3 pattern of making, and being accountable for, specific commitments to do and share. But legalism occurs when person A tells person B what they should do, and criticizes them if they don't (as the Pharisees criticized Jesus concerning the sabbath). That is not what happens in a 3/3 group. In a 3/3 group, each individual prays and asks God what He wants them to do in response to the passage. Then, each individual shares with the group their personal plan.

At the following meeting, the group checks on how each of its members implemented their respective plans. It is not person A holding person B accountable for what person A thinks God wants. Person B is held accountable for what he or she has heard God say to them and has shared with their spiritual community. The emphasis is not on some external standard of behavior, but on each person's heart before the Lord. By holding its members accountable, the group is doing its utmost to love each person, because they know that the only path to joy is to do and share what God says.

PRAYER

O Lord, above all You value radical, immediate, costly obedience. Help me move in that direction. And help me help others move in that direction too. Only if I keep Your commands can I abide in Your love. And that's where I want to be. Wrench out, by the roots, the things that hold me back. In Jesus' name, Amen.

QUESTIONS

Read the following questions, then pray and ask God what He wants you to learn and do. Listen quietly.

Review your journal. Are there any past commitments you have not completed? If needed, schedule revised completion dates.

1. Am I weakest in knowing, doing, or sharing? How can I strengthen my areas of weakness?

2. Am I telling new believers what to believe, or training them to learn for themselves? How can I do less of the first and more of the second?

3. How can I integrate the 3/3 pattern into my life?

4. What specific actions does God want me to take in response to this chapter? (Note them in your journal and schedule them in your calendar.)

5. With whom (at least one name) does God want me to share what I have learned?

Ask the Lord to enable you to follow through on these commitments and to prepare the hearts of those with whom you intend to share insights.

15 Living Accountable Lives

Constant accountability is crucial in your daily experience
of knowing and following the Lord.

He who is faithful in a very little thing is faithful also in much; and he
who is unrighteous in a very little thing is unrighteous also in much.

—LUKE 16:10

The Christian life is like a diet or a fitness program. Deciding to eat one
hamburger will hardly cause me gain weight. My fitness (or lack thereof)
results from thousands of small decisions. In the same way, spiritual
growth (or the lack of it) results from a repeated cycle of learning, doing,
and sharing (or not). Daily habits are the bricks that build the house of
your life. I want to share habits that I and many others find helpful in
building a Theopraxic life. Two helpful habits are daily Scripture reading
and journaling and weekly conversations with an accountability partner.

In my daily personal time in Scripture, I read four to five chapters—a
minimum of twenty-five chapters per week. From each day's reading,
I select one to four verses that the Lord particularly impresses upon me.
Then I record insights in my journal regarding those few verses, using the
acrostic SOAPS:

Scripture (Write the verses)

Observation (Write the main idea or paraphrase the verses)

Application (Determine what the Lord wants me to do or be or change)

Prayer (Write a prayer regarding the application)

Share (Write any person or persons with whom I will share the insight)

In addition, I talk regularly (usually weekly, on the phone or a video call) with an accountability partner. We discuss what the Lord has been showing us, how it has impacted us, whom we have been sharing with, and a whole range of general life accountability questions.

The accountability questions cover broad, ongoing issues related to living a sanctified life. They serve as an early warning system to alert me to areas where I am starting to walk in the flesh rather than in the Spirit. They help me recognize issues of concern before they become habitual or entrenched. Where issues arise, I can confess them to God and to my accountability partner and deal with them before they become major problems (JAMES 5:16).

An accountability partner should be of the same gender as you and committed to growing in his or her relationship with God. There also needs to be a mutual understanding of confidentiality. You can agree together on what passages of Scripture to read each week. During your meeting time, you will go over a set of questions regarding your life since you last met.

The questions I use are similar to those used by John Wesley, the founder of Methodism, in his famous accountability groups, and by my good friend Neil Cole in his Life Transformation Groups (LTGs).

Here are the questions I use:

1. How have your insights from last week's reading shaped the way you think and live?

2. With whom did you share your insights from last week, and how was it received?

3. How have you seen God at work?

4. Have you been a testimony this week to the greatness of Jesus Christ with both your words and actions?

5. Have you been exposed to sexually alluring material or allowed your mind to entertain inappropriate sexual thoughts?

6. Have you acknowledged God's ownership in your use of money?

7. Have you coveted anything?

8. Have you hurt someone's reputation or feelings by your words?

9. Have you been dishonest or exaggerated anything in your words or actions?

10. Have you given in to an addictive (or lazy or undisciplined) behavior?

11. Have you been a slave to clothing, friends, work, or possessions?

12. Have you failed to forgive someone?

13. What worries or anxieties are you facing? Have you complained or grumbled? Have you maintained a thankful heart?

14. Have you been honoring, understanding, and generous in your important relationships?

15. What temptations in thought, word, or action have you faced, and how did you respond?

16. How have you taken opportunities to serve or bless others, especially believers?

17. Have you seen specific answers to prayer?

18. Did you complete the reading for the week?

Sometimes, in areas with low literacy levels, it will be necessary to make adjustments to these daily and weekly patterns. Instead of the list of questions, I ask people to memorize a few passages of Scripture (such as GALATIANS 5:19–23; 1 JOHN 2:15–16; 1 CORINTHIANS 13:4–7; 2 TIMOTHY 3:16–17) and use them as the basis for discussing issues of spiritual accountability. Rather than reading twenty-five or more chapters of Scripture per week, they listen to Scripture on their phones or an audio Bible.

As we discussed in the previous chapter, a large volume of Bible reading is essential to learn practical hermeneutics (i.e., Bible interpretation and application skills). One goal for every disciple of the Lord is to learn to interpret and apply Scripture for themselves. That is impossible without broad exposure to the Bible as a whole.

If you use the 3/3 pattern in your weekly church meetings, you are receiving regular doses of detailed examination of short passages. Using the 3/3 approach with a group of eight people typically takes about three hours to cover around twenty verses. Multi-chapter sessions are just not practical.

No amount of deep digging into brief passages will ever result in a well-rounded toolkit for interpreting Scripture. To pick up on important cues, such as the influence of the genre, clues about the original audience, the impact of context, and skill in comparing and contrasting passages, it is essential to take in large chunks of Scripture. You can learn about these aspects of biblical interpretation by hearing sermons or reading books, but to learn to interpret Scripture well for yourself you need to ingest longer passages. I can assure you that those who write or speak about key insights have done that. Notably, no other person can tell you exactly how the Lord wants you to apply Scripture. That can only come directly from Him. Being saturated with Scripture gives You a better foundation from which to hear Him.

It is certainly possible to consume large chunks of Scripture thoughtlessly, which is why the SOAPS approach is helpful. It helps to maintain a level of focus and an eye toward application as you complete your daily reading. It also provides an opportunity for a brief "deeper dive" each day.

I urge keeping a journal so that you can capture what you hear the Lord teaching you and encouraging you to apply and share with others. The act of writing will help sink this into your mind. It will also permit you to review the journal from time to time to check for any unfinished commitments. If you have a perfect memory, then you don't need a journal for this purpose. If you are like the rest of us and want to take seriously what the Lord impresses on you, then you need a journal. Once you have done what He asked you to do, you never need to look at it again. Until you do what He asked, you need a reminder.

Remember, the ongoing issues and general principles will be dealt with in the accountability meetings. The journal is aimed more at the specific applications you ask the Holy Spirit to highlight in your 3/3 meetings and SOAPS readings.

As much as possible, the application items in the 3/3 process and SOAPS journaling should be framed as specific and observable applications, not principle-based concepts. We want to make a plan of action, not articulate a wish. It is more powerful to make a clear commitment, like "I will help my wife wash the dishes tonight," than to say, "I should be more considerate of others."

Initially, this may seem difficult, especially for people who have been Christians for a while. We are used to hearing principle-based applications from sermons and teaching. This is necessary because pastors and teachers need to make generic applications that are applicable to everyone. What we are seeking is instruction from the Lord on how He wants us personally to apply those general principles or concepts in our lives. This is an essential step in terms of learning to hear His voice and identifying actions for which we can be held accountable.

PRAYER

Lord, help me to be faithful in the little things. Help me to build habits into my life to establish a virtuous cycle of learn, do, share, and repeat. Show me, specifically, what changes You want me to make in my daily and weekly routine.

QUESTIONS

Read the following questions, then pray and ask God what He wants you to learn and do. Listen quietly.

Review your journal. Are there any past commitments you have not completed? If needed, schedule revised completion dates.

1. Do my daily and weekly habits hold me accountable to grow in faithfulness? Which of the tools in this chapter might be helpful for me to use?

2. What specific actions does God want me to take in response to this chapter? (Note them in your journal and schedule them in your calendar.)

3. With whom (at least one name) does God want me to share what I have learned?

Ask the Lord to enable you to follow through on these commitments and to prepare the hearts of those with whom you intend to share insights.

16 Growing in Prayer

We need to grow toward a life of constant prayer.

> They were continually devoting themselves to the apostles' teaching and to fellowship, to the breaking of bread and to prayer.
>
> —ACTS 2:42

Prayer is conversation with God. It is an essential aspect of getting to know Him more intimately. Our conversations with Him reveal a lot about the nature of our relationship with Him. A good conversation with God involves a lot of listening. I must listen so I can understand and do His will. This is the fabric of life in Christ. In this chapter, I will discuss three tools to improve your prayer life.

Prayerwalking teaches us to see things from God's perspective. It is the best way I know to grow in that ability. It also allows us to practice recognizing the voice of the Holy Spirit and to obey Jesus' command to pray that God's will be done on earth as it is in heaven (MATTHEW 6:10).

Prayerwalking means praying while you walk, usually about things you see as you walk. It is best to prayerwalk with a partner. This creates a three-way conversation between you, your friend, and the Lord. In this way, you gain a double advantage—hearing directly from the Lord and also hearing how the Lord is speaking to the other person. Often, as a result, your prayers build on one another's prayers and go in directions that neither of you would have contemplated if you had prayed alone.

There are generally four ways to determine what to pray for when prayerwalking:

1.   Observation
2.   Revelation
3.   Research
4.   Praying based on a passage of Scripture

Observation means that you pray about what you see, hear, or smell as you are walking. For example, if you are in a residential neighborhood and see a tricycle in a yard, that might prompt you to pray for the family life in that home, or for children in the neighborhood, or even for people's transportation needs.

Revelation refers to God putting something in your mind—something apparently unrelated to what you are observing. Sometimes this can be in the form of a picture, but often it is simply a topic or thought.

We can also pray about issues we have learned of by conducting research. For example, you might have read of problems with unemployment, teenage pregnancy, or drug abuse. Then, as you walk through the neighborhood, you can pray for those issues. Research, obviously, requires preplanning and intentionality.

Praying based on a passage of Scripture can be planned in advance, or you may be led to a particular passage during a prayerwalk. This is more likely to happen if you are deeply familiar with Scripture.

In practical terms, we are looking for the gaps between God's will and the situation on earth. In the Lord's Prayer, Jesus taught us to pray, "Your will be done, on earth as it is in heaven" (MATTHEW 6:10). As we walk, we are noting specific areas where God's will is *not* being done and asking God to do it, making ourselves available for Him to use in His answer to the prayer. When we prayerwalk, we engage in a conversation with God, asking Him to reveal what He thinks about what we are observing. You can ask God questions about what you are seeing as you prayerwalk, and He can guide you into conversations with and prayers for people you encounter. All these experiences increase our capacity to hear God and see situations from His perspective.

With practice, this can become habitual, and we can begin to experience *prayerliving* rather than praying only at special times and places. This is what Paul meant when he commanded us to "pray without ceasing" (1 Thessalonians 5:17). Prayerwalking teaches us to see the world as God sees it. This is central to being Theopraxic.

Our attitude toward prayer should be like our attitude toward air or water or food. We simply cannot do without it. Jesus certainly had this perspective. He said His food was to do the Father's will and accomplish His work (John 4:34). He said that man does not live on bread alone, but on every word God speaks (Matthew 4:4). How can we hear every word if we are not constantly listening? Prayer is not an incidental practice, but a constant manner of life to be cultivated.

It is possible to pray in ways that have no value. Jesus warns that those who pray in public, "so that they may be seen by men," will receive no reward from the Father (Matthew 6:5–6). Prayer is not intended to be a public display, but a personal interaction with God. If we are aware of being in His presence, it is difficult to ignore Him. Imagine standing before an earthly king. Would you completely ignore him? No, you would pay close attention to his attitude toward whatever you were doing or saying. We should do the same when we are in God's presence (which is always). We earnestly desire to know what He thinks about our actions, speech, and attitudes.

Frequently, we may not know what to pray. When I feel like this, I assume that I am better off remaining silent and listening. Sometimes this feeling means that it is time to ask a question. If we are supposed to say something to God in prayer, we have the unimaginable benefit of the Holy Spirit interceding on our behalf with groans that are beyond words, and the Father hears and understands perfectly (Romans 8:26).

Often, especially in this over-busy world, it is difficult to maintain focus when we pray. It is easy to be distracted. I would like to mention one other practical resource: the prayer wheel, developed by Dick Eastman at Every Home for Christ. (Used by permission. Dick Eastman, *The Hour that Changes the World*, Grand Rapids, MI: Chosen Books, 2002). It is a simple way to spend an undistracted hour in prayer. It is divided into twelve sections, each for a different type of prayer (as listed below). The goal is to use each section as a guide for five minutes of prayer. Together, the twelve segments result in a helpful guide for an hour of prayer.

How to pray for one hour using the prayer wheel:

1. **PRAISE:** Start your prayer hour by praising the Lord. Praise Him for things that are on your mind right now. Praise Him for one special thing He has done in your life in the past week. Praise Him for His goodness to your family. (Psalm 34:1)

2. **WAITING:** Spend this time waiting on the Lord. Let Him pull together reflections for you. Think about the hour before you and the things you want the Lord to do in your life. (Psalm 27:14)

3. **CONFESSION:** Ask the Holy Spirit to show you anything in your life which might be displeasing to Him. Ask Him to point out attitudes that are wrong, as well as specific acts for which you have not yet made a prayer of confession. Now confess that to the Lord and claim 1 John 1:9 so that you might be cleansed for the remainder of the hour before you, and then pick up and read the Word. (Psalm 51:1–19)

4. **PRAYERFULLY READ THE WORD:** Spend time reading promises of God in the Psalms, in the prophets, and passages on prayer located in the New Testament. Check your concordance. (PSALM 119:97)

5. **PETITION:** This is general request for others, praying through the prayer list, the prayer cards, or personal prayer interest on behalf of yourself and others. (HEBREWS 4:16)

6. **INTERCESSION:** Specific prayer on the behalf of others. Pray specifically for those requests of which you are aware. (ROMANS 15:30–33)

7. **PRAY THE WORD:** Now take the Scriptures and start praying the Scriptures. Certain sections of PSALM 119 lend themselves beautifully to prayer expression. (PSALM 119:38–46)

8. **THANKSGIVING:** Spend these minutes giving thanks to the Lord for things in your life, things on behalf of the church, your extended family, your workplace, and your community. (Philippians 4:6)

9. **SINGING:** Take your hymnal and sing a prayer song, sing a praise song, sing a song regarding soul winning or witnessing. Let it be a time of praise. (PSALM 59:17)

10. **MEDITATE ON THE WORD:** Ask the Lord to speak to you. Keep a paper and pen handy, ready to relate the impressions that He makes upon your life. (PSALM 63)

11. **LISTEN:** Spend time merging the things you have read from the Word, the things you have prayed, the things you have thanked the Lord for, and the things that you have been singing, and see how the Lord brings them all together to speak to you. (1 SAMUEL 3:9–10)

12. **END WITH PRAISE:** Praise the Lord for the time you have had to spend with Him. Praise Him for the impressions that He has given you. Praise Him for the prayer requests He raised up in your mind. (PSALM 145:1–13)

People, especially in the United States, have limited attention spans and, therefore, a limited capacity for prayer. The prayer wheel offers an effective way for many to increase their capacity. It also helps people to have a more balanced approach to their prayer life—especially with regard to listening more, which is a critical aspect of following the Lord.

An additional prayer practice that I have found surprisingly fruitful is praying for my enemies. We all know that part of God's upside-down Kingdom is the command to love our enemies and pray for those who persecute us. Three times in my life, people have egregiously wronged me in ways that upended my life. Fortunately, in retrospect I can look back and clearly discern how the Lord used each of those situations for my good. That is not always the case in this life. Many such traumatic events can be properly understood only in eternity.

In any case, I make it a discipline to pray for each of those three people daily. I pray in a way related to my "Application" item for that day's SOAPS journal entry. (Incidentally, I do the same for many other people who are on my daily prayer list.) For example, I recently read LUKE 21:34–36, where Jesus says,

> Be on guard, so that your hearts will not be weighted down with dissipation and drunkenness and the worries of life, and that day will not come on you suddenly like a trap; for it will come upon all those who dwell on the face of all the earth. But keep on the alert at all times, praying that you may have strength to escape all these things that are about to take place, and to stand before the Son of Man.

The generalized application was that we are to avoid anything that would weaken or distract us from being alert for Christ's return or from being ready for the difficulties that will precede His return. We are also to pray for strength to endure those difficulties. As I prayed for the people on my prayer list, I asked the Lord what particular aspects of that application would be relevant and helpful for each individual, and then I prayed toward that end.

Frequently, my daily prayers for those three "enemies" concerning that day's application give me additional insights into nuances of the application that I would not have noticed had I been praying only for myself or others who are close to me. These prayers give me an awareness of dimensions of virtue, corruption, motivation, and temptation that would never occur to me otherwise. I am constantly astonished at the impact this simple habit has on me. I am deeply blessed by it. It also helps me better understand and love the people I am praying for.

Prayer brings together the topics of listening and unity. Prayer is intended to be a corporate practice as well as an individual one. The Lord's Prayer, in MATTHEW 6:9–13, is in the plural: "Our Father ... our daily bread ... forgive us our debts ... do not lead us ... deliver us." Many of the instructions for prayer in the epistles are in the plural as well.

Based on John's emphases on love, listening, and unity, it is no surprise that he gives his well-known prayer promise in the plural in 1 JOHN 5:14–15:

> This is the confidence which we have before Him, that, if we ask anything according to His will, He hears us. And if we know that He hears us *in whatever we ask, we know that we have the requests which we have asked from Him.*

This means that we should invest time in praying with one another. It also means that we should pray for one another and in agreement with each other. There is a particular significance to praying in this way. We see an example of that in MATTHEW 18:19–20, where Jesus says, "Again I say to you, that if two of you agree on earth about anything that they may ask, it shall be done for them by My Father who is in heaven. For where two or three have gathered together in My name, I am there in their midst."

The matters about which we can be most confident of God's will in our individual and corporate prayers are those that directly impinge upon God's glory and greatness being made known and His Kingdom being advanced. This is a major purpose of God. Moses (NUMBERS 14:11–19), Daniel (DANIEL 9:1–19), and other faithful saints have understood this aspect of prayer. We would do well to make that the primary direction of our prayers also.

This is a major consideration in prayer. God will act according to His own purposes. John makes this clear in 1 JOHN 5:14–15, as quoted above: If we pray *according to His will*, we can have confidence about what we are requesting from Him. The more we know the Lord and understand His will, character, and ways, the more confidently and powerfully we can pray.

PRAYER

Lord, forgive me. My lack of prayer stems from my lack of belief. I don't pray much because I don't really believe that I can do nothing without You. I don't really believe that You hear and care and answer. Forgive me. Teach me to go through life praying without ceasing. Teach me to constantly listen for Your voice and seek Your perspective on all that is going on around me. Help me fight through the distractions and focus on You. Teach me to pray.

QUESTIONS

Read the following questions, then pray and ask God what He wants you to learn and do. Listen quietly.

Review your journal. Are there any past commitments you have not completed? If needed, schedule revised completion dates.

1. Would I benefit from practicing prayerwalking, the prayer wheel, and praying for my enemies? How will I incorporate those activities into my regular routines?

2. What specific actions does God want me to take in response to this chapter? (Note them in your journal and schedule them in your calendar.)

3. With whom (at least one name) does God want me to share what I have learned?

Ask the Lord to enable you to follow through on these commitments and to prepare the hearts of those with whom you intend to share insights.

17 Training Disciples to Make Disciples

We need to utilize the training cycle in order to intentionally work toward making disciples who make disciples.

The things which you have heard from me in the presence of many witnesses, entrust these to faithful men who will be able to teach others also.

—2 TIMOTHY 2:2

Being a follower of Christ implies making followers of Christ. Matthew's Gospel concludes with Jesus' final instructions to His disciples, known as the Great Commission (MATTHEW 28:18–20). He told them, "All authority has been given to Me in heaven and on earth. Go therefore and make disciples of all the nations, baptizing them in the name of the Father and the Son and the Holy Spirit, teaching them to observe all that I commanded you; and lo, I am with you always, even to the end of the age."

In a sense, the Great Commission is Jesus' summary command. The primary verb, the imperative verb, is "make disciples." The other verbs (go, baptize, teach) are actually participles in the original Greek, and they describe *how* we are to make disciples. One of those descriptors is "teaching them to observe [obey] all that I commanded you." Hence, we make disciples by teaching them to obey all of Jesus' commands. The output of the disciple-making process should be disciples who obey Jesus' commands. And, of course, one of the commands of Jesus is to make disciples. So an obedient disciple is, by definition, a disciple-making disciple.

How can we effectively do that? How can we make disciples who obey Jesus' commands, including His command to make disciples? How can we ensure that we are learning to obey all of Christ's commands and to teach that same discipline to others, who will in turn teach it to others? How can we do this in such a way that the process will continue for spiritual generation after spiritual generation?

The MAWL training cycle is one helpful pattern to accomplish this. MAWL is an acrostic describing the four phases of the training cycle: Model, Assist, Watch, Leave.

Let's look at an example: training someone to ride a bicycle. This follows the four phases of MAWL. Modeling does not take long, but it is necessary. Before people can learn to ride a bike, they need to see somebody else riding one. The role of a model is to create the concept of what is being taught. This happens the moment a person sees someone else riding a bicycle. In the modeling phase, the trainer performs the skill and the trainee watches.

The "assist" phase is a bit longer. Here, the trainee is the one on the bicycle, but the trainer is there to help—perhaps walking alongside the cyclist with one hand on the handlebars and the other on the seat. This phase can be relatively short, giving the learner a basic understanding of what it feels like to ride. We don't want to assist for too long, lest we develop a pattern of dependence.

The "watch" phase is far longer. The learner is now developing independence as the instructor introduces additional skills and some of the finer points of riding: how to mount a bicycle, how to start from a standstill, how to steer around obstacles and curves, how to brake, how to go uphill and downhill, where and when it is safe to ride, how to obey traffic laws and follow traffic patterns, etc.

Once the learner has mastered all the basics, the instructor can *leave*. The newly trained bicycle rider can ride independently and can even begin teaching others how to ride.

We could describe the four stages of the training cycle as developmental levels. People at level 1 need a model. At level 2, they need hands-on assistance and guidance. Level 3 learners need more refinement in their application or understanding. Level 4 means that they have mastered the basic skills and are able to teach others.

Of course, people are not at the same level of development in everything they do—their level varies depending on the skill. I am at level 1 in gene splicing, level 2 in yodeling, level 3 in playing the harmonica, and level 4 as a scuba diver, since I am professionally certified to train other divers.

Generally, people can train someone who is at least one developmental level below them in that particular skill. Because teaching a skill is one of the best ways to learn that skill better, we encourage people to participate in teaching as soon as they reach level 2.

Mentoring someone through the training cycle requires flexibility on the part of the mentor. At level 1, people need clear direction. At level 2, they need clear direction plus encouragement. At level 3, they need encouragement but much less direction. Specifically, they should be encouraged to take the initiative with regard to the topics and pace of their further growth. Level 4 people have few needs other than the fellowship of other practitioners.

The time length of the equipping roles differs: Modeling should be very short, assisting relatively short, and watching quite long. The first two phases are face-to-face and intensive in most cases. The watching phase can often be managed at a distance, especially with the electronic communication devices available today, and it is more ad hoc in nature.

Finally, if I am mentoring someone in a range of related concepts and skills, then I use a coaching checklist. Once I believe that the trainee has reached level 3 on all the skills, I give the checklist to the trainee, who then rates himself or herself on each skill. This helps me to ensure that the learner is ready to take charge of the remainder of the equipping process and confirms that we are in agreement as to how much progress has been made.

See the following chart for the coaching checklist I use in my discipling. Don't be concerned with the specific topics in the left column. Those are merely illustrative and can be adapted for your personal approach.

COACHING CHECKLIST

	Model UNAWARE Train with new information and make sure of understanding.	Assist UNSKILLED Stop and stay with them until they have the basics.	Watch COMPETENT Watch out for consistent competence.	Leave SKILLED Go ahead and leave them and find others to develop.
	Mentor's Role			
	Mentor gives Direction & Information	Mentor gives Direction & Support	Mentor gives Support & Encouragement	Mentor receives Updates
	How Plans are Made			
TRAINING TOOL	Mentor Decides	Mentor/ee Discuss Mentor Decides	Mentor/ee Discuss Mentee Decides	Mentee Decides
Duckling Discipleship				
Tell Your Story [Testimony]				
Stewardship of Relationships–List of 100				
Pace				
Non-Sequential Ministry				
3/3 Group Format				
Simple Church–Love God/Others, Make Disciples				
Being Part of Two Churches				
Training Cycle				
Accountability Groups				
Self-Feeding:				
–Reading the Word Daily [Obey]				
–Prayer–Talk & Listen [Prayer Cycle]				
–Body Life–Fellowship [One Another's]				
–Persecution & Suffering				
Eyes to See Where the Kingdom Isn't				
Looking for the Person of Peace [Mt. 10, Lk. 10]				
Prayer Walking				
Being a Church:				
–Fellowship [Eat Together, One Another's]				
–Praise & Worship				
–Bible [Obey, Train]				
–Telling People about Jesus [Share]				
–Baptism				

In situations where the cluster of skills and concepts is complex, a worksheet like this one helps to ensure that the entire set of abilities is passed on in its entirety and that the skills, abilities, and attitudes of succeeding generations remain consistent. Also, if you are mentoring several people, it helps to remind you what you have and have not covered with each one.

Once a person has achieved level 4 in all relevant skills, then the mentoring relationship ends and a peer-to-peer relationship begins. Mastering the training cycle itself is almost always the last item on which a person achieves developmental level 4. The reason why people need to be at the fourth generation of reproduction to "graduate" is that only then have they demonstrated their ability to successfully carry out each of the roles of being a trainer. They need to appropriately leave generation 1 after generation 1 is watching generation 2; meanwhile, generation 2 is assisting generation 3 and generation 3 is modeling for generation 4. This takes a while, especially with complex clusters of skills and concepts. Most people don't do it well the first time, and training must be carried out effectively through all four generations.

Implementing the training cycle is an important skill not only in disciple making but in any training or equipping that we hope to see reproduced to multiple generations. Doing it well requires discipline. If someone you are mentoring proves to be unmotivated and unfaithful to the process, then you should not invest a large amount of time in that person. Invest instead in those who are faithful in applying and passing on what you give them. *Invest deeply in the few in such a way that they do the same with others.* The fruit harvested from such an approach will be abundant within a few generations.

I strongly suggest that you go through the Zúme training online to gain experience in the training cycle and other tools I have introduced. Zúme means yeast in Greek. In MATTHEW 13:33, Jesus said, "The kingdom of heaven is like leaven, which a woman took and hid in three pecks of flour until it was all leavened." This illustrates how ordinary people, using ordinary resources, can have an extraordinary impact for the Kingdom of God.

Zúme is a free online introductory training on how to multiply disciples and simple churches. It can be found at zumeproject.com. It is being translated into forty languages so that it can be used in most parts of the world. By participating in Zúme, you will have access to a coach who can

guide you through the process of implementing what you have learned
and answer any questions you may have.

Once you have begun to practice these patterns, you may want to
become part of 24:14 (2414now.net), a coalition that derives its name
from MATTHEW 24:14: "This gospel of the kingdom shall be preached in
the whole world as a testimony to all the nations, and then the end will
come." The 24:14 practitioners have banded together and are working
collaboratively to ensure that multiplicative approaches to disciple making
are being implemented in every place and among every people group
globally by the end of 2025. The 24:14 network is a good place to get
more advanced training and coaching as you progress in your disciple-
making journey.

Finally, because it is an integral part of making disciples, it is helpful to
give detailed thought to what exactly are all the commands Christ gave.
I would encourage you to read the "Commands of Christ" blog series,
which is one of the documents available for free download at obeygc2.com.
It covers a multitude of specific practical areas of life. Examining our own
lives in the light of those specific commands is a helpful practice.

PRAYER

Heavenly Father, You have given me the job of making disciples who obey You and who will make more disciples. Help me to do it well. Bring me to faithful people. Help me train them as Jesus trained the Twelve. Give me patience, but not too much patience, because I want to maintain a holy dissatisfaction with the status quo. Give me faithfulness, sacrifice, and discipline. Teach me to teach them to teach others, for the expansion of Your Kingdom and for the praise of Your glory!

QUESTIONS

Read the following questions, then pray and ask God what He wants you to learn and do. Listen quietly.

Review your journal. Are there any past commitments you have not completed? If needed, schedule revised completion dates.

1. Am I intentionally making disciples? If not, with whom should I start doing so? If so, in which aspects of the training cycle am I the most deficient? How can I begin to improve in this phase?

2. What specific actions does God want me to take in response to this chapter? (Note them in your journal and schedule them in your calendar.)

3. With whom (at least one name) does God want me to share what I have learned?

Ask the Lord to enable you to follow through on these commitments and to prepare the hearts of those with whom you intend to share insights.

ADDITIONAL RESOURCES

WEBSITES

zumeproject.com—Zúme is a free introductory online training for multiplying disciples and simple churches. Ten two-hour sessions. Small-group design. Video-based. Coaching provided. Available in multiple languages. Soon zume.training and zume.vision.

metacamp.org—Website for our missions and disciple-making training center in Dadeville, Alabama. My blog also appears on this website. Check the training calendar for a suitable opportunity or request a training event in your area.

2414now.net—A coalition of practitioners committed to seeing teams that use multiplicative disciple-making approaches operating in every part of the world and with every people group by 2025.

multiplyingdisciples.learnnn.com—Some additional disciple-making training topics. The quality of design in the videos is not high, but the content is helpful.

obeygc2.com—My personal website. Information about this book and other downloads is available here. *You can get a coupon for a free version of the ebook and audio book on this site.*

DOWNLOADS

4 Relationships video (https://www.youtube.com/watch?v=dvIvArV_Zf0) tells the history of humankind from creation to new creation in Christ and promotes Zúme as an outreach method.

Author's testimony (https://zume.life/testimony-1/) about some of the issues in this book.

Blessing Booklet (https://zume.life/wp-content/uploads/2019/02/Blessing-booklet.pdf)—This is a resource that we used with our children to help them develop a life of Theopraxy. (31.9 MB)

Scenic Psalms (https://zume.life/wp-content/uploads/2019/02/Scenic-Psalms-2-page-view.pdf)—This is a pictorial representation of some verses from the Psalms. (24.3 MB) To view it properly, in Adobe Reader select "View," then "Page Display," then "Two-Up." This is purely for enjoyment and encouragement.

More Disciples (found on Amazon) is the only resource on this list that is not free of charge. This book, written by Doug Lucas, goes into more detail on the tools mentioned in the third section of this book. There is a related website (**moredisciples.com**) as well. All sales proceeds go to the Zúme project.

ABOUT THE AUTHOR

DR. CURTIS SERGEANT served with the International Mission Board (IMB) as a pioneer church-planting missionary among an unreached people group in China. When the work began to produce rapidly multiplying churches and he was no longer needed there, Curtis transitioned to a ministry of training others to do the same sort of ministry. In that role, he intensively trained hundreds of people from a wide range of nations, denominations, and agencies, who have collectively catalyzed movements that have planted millions of house churches.

A few years later, Curtis began to interface with the major house-church networks of China as a trainer and consultant. Later, he served as the IMB's vice president for global strategy, where he oversaw the research department while continuing to fulfill a training role as well.

From there, Curtis went to Saddleback Church as the director of church planting. While at Saddleback, he helped to develop an online training system for missions and led some extremely large-scale church-planting projects, especially in India. During that period, he was also instrumental in initiating church-planting ministry among nearly a hundred previously unengaged people groups. Curtis then served as international vice president of e3 Partners for three years.

Curtis currently operates MetaCamp, a disciple-making and missions-training center located in Dadeville, Alabama. He also works in leadership with Zúme and 24:14. Curtis and his wife, Debie, have two grown and married children, Nathan and Megan.

APPENDIX 1:
KINGDOM ORISONS

This part of the book contains prayers that I have composed during my own devotional times, covering a wide range of spiritual concerns related to living a life of Theopraxy. I have arranged them in a set of thirty daily readings so that you can pray through the whole set in one month.

Let me briefly explain the title of the collection. I call them *Kingdom* Orisons because they are focused primarily on the Kingdom of heaven and on God as our King. That, of course, is not the only topic to pray about. All topics that affect our lives, from the sublime to the seemingly insignificant, could be worthy of prayer. Our Creator is concerned with every part of our lives, even the number of hairs on our head. These prayers, however, focus on coming to understand the Kingdom and our place in it as citizens and on appreciating our King more fully. For some people, this tends to be a relatively neglected aspect of prayer.

The word *orisons* is simply a synonym for "prayers." It is admittedly archaic, but that is by design. Through God's new covenant with us in Jesus Christ, we understand that we are children of God and even friends of God. Prayer thus becomes an intimate experience. We can and should be in constant conversation with the ruler of the universe! Some people, however, develop a casual or even cavalier attitude toward prayer over time.

I have used the word *orisons* to catch readers' attention because of its unfamiliarity. The prayers themselves are also somewhat formal in nature—more so than my typical daily prayers—because I want to foster a sense of wonder and reverence. Although God is indeed intimate with us, He is also wholly other and ineffable. These prayers are intended to remind us of that aspect of His being.

My hope is that these prayers from my heart may refresh your heart, draw you closer to our eternal King and His Kingdom, and intensify your love for Him and your desire to use every moment, every encounter, every opportunity, to know and glorify Him more fully. May God use your life to encourage those around you to take their next step on a spiritual journey that will glorify the Lord and bring joy to His heart.

I do not claim to pray better than anyone else, but you may find these prayers helpful in bringing various aspects of Christian devotion to mind, or as a starting point to enable you to formulate more specific prayers for the people or situations in your own life.

Day 1

Savior of all grace, produce in me the faith to live in You, desiring nothing else—with You as all my hope, all my aim, all my glory. May You be both my path and my guide, both my model to imitate and the potter who shapes me.

You are my foundation and refuge. You are the prophet who instructs me, the priest who intercedes for me, and the king who rules me. May I rely entirely on You, and may I love and serve You with all my heart, mind, soul, and strength.

May I never be ashamed of You or Your words, but joyfully bear any opposition or sacrifice that comes as a result of faithfully following You; and may I count it a privilege and glory to be so identified with You.

May I avoid bringing sorrow to Your heart by any failure through omission or commission. Let me never retreat or delay when You bid me to advance. Let me be so attentive to Your desires and direction that a mere glance from You will result in my full and complete response.

Keep me from this present evil world and its influences. Protect me from its allures, intimidations, vices, and errors. Infuse my heart with so much love for You that there is no room left for love of anything else, including the lust of the eyes, the lust of the flesh, and the boastful pride of life.

Constantly remind me that I am a citizen of Your Kingdom and only a stranger passing through this world. Let me seek that country and Your reign, continually expressing Your will and Your ways more fully in word and deed and serving as a faithful ambassador, calling others to submit to You as the all-wise and all-good King.

By faith may I more clearly perceive Your voice and Your activity in my life and in the world. Each day may I more clearly understand Your will on earth in order that I might pursue it until that day when it is done here as in heaven. Be glorified in me and through me, I pray.

Prayer of Confession Inspired by the Early Church Fathers

Heavenly Father, You made my body to serve You and my soul to follow hard after You. With sorrow and contrition of heart, I admit before You my faults and my failures.

My failure to be true even to my own accepted standards;
My self-deception in the face of temptation;
My choosing of the worse when I know the better;
O Lord, forgive!

My silence when You would have me speak and my speech when You would have me keep silent;
My actions when You would have me wait on You and my hesitation when You would have me act;
My complacency toward wrongs that do not affect me and my oversensitivity to those that do;
O Lord, forgive!

My lack of Your compassion in showing mercy for the downtrodden and the lost;
My pride in considering my own comfort and convenience above the needs of others;
My blindness to the suffering of others and my slowness to be taught by my own;
O Lord, forgive!

My failure to apply to myself the standards of conduct I demand of others;
My slowness to see the good in others and to see the evil in myself;
My hardness of heart toward my neighbors' faults and my readiness to make allowance for my own;
O Lord, forgive!

My unwillingness to recognize that You have called me to a small work and my brother to a great one;
My ingratitude and grumbling when You place a great opportunity before me to display Your grace;
My failure to recognize Your loving hand in all that touches me;
O Lord, forgive!

Day 2

Holy Lord, forgive me. I find that my entire life continues to be tainted by pride and unbelief. I fail to see You as I should in all Your holiness, power, love, and goodness, or to live in the light of that understanding. As a result, I perceive myself wrongly. I compare myself to other wretched creatures rather than to You and the beauty and perfection that You deserve and demand. As a result, I err in my desires, my goals, my standards, my self-perception, and my daily living.

Please complete the good work You have begun in me. Transform and renew my mind so that I might perceive You in all Your glory and then think rightly of myself and others. Let me rely on and submit to Your righteousness so that I might be conformed to the image of Christ. Rule my mind, my body, my soul, and my spirit entirely, and purge from me the attractions of other things that tempt me to live for anything but You.

Thank You for Your loving work in me, whether through the joy of fellowship with You through prayer, Scripture, and Your body, or through the refining fires of suffering that You send to bless me and prepare me for fuller joy in Your presence. Do not spare me from any trial that would make me more pleasing to You or bring You greater glory. Remove anything from me that dims the brightness of Your grace or hinders me from rejoicing in You.

Prayer for Protection from the "Spiritual" Versions of the Seven Deadly Sins

Lord, I realize that even though by Your grace I have become relatively immune to temptations that used to cause me great difficulty, I am still subject to "spiritual" versions of the same types of temptation. I know that these new versions are not benign, but require constant vigilance on my part if I am to avoid sin in these areas.

Pride: Lord, I realize that spiritual pride is, if anything, more egregious than carnal pride, because it robs You of even more glory. Protect my heart from any temptation to think that anything good comes from me apart from Your work through me. I know that any virtue or righteousness comes from You. I know that any spiritual gift I have is from You. I know that any fruit in ministry comes from You. I know that any way others are blessed by me is from You. Let me not think of myself, but of You and others. Let me not consider myself better than others. You are the vine. I am simply a branch. I can do nothing apart from You.

Greed: Lord, protect me from spiritual greed. Just as greed for temporal things leads to pursuit of more things than one needs, so spiritual greed can tempt me to pursue more than You have ordained in spiritual matters. I can desire more admiration for ministry, more spiritual gifts than I can steward well, and more influence than I have the wisdom to use for the good of others and for Your glory. Let me concern myself with wisely stewarding the gifts and influence You have given me. Help me to be concerned with the depth of my ministry and to let You be concerned with the breadth of it.

Lust: Lord, protect me from spiritual lust, from desiring what You have chosen that I should not have. Do not let me be tempted by lust for credit or glory. Do not let me lust for power or authority over others in matters of Your Kingdom. Let me love You rather than the benefits You bless me with or the gifts You give.

Envy: Lord, protect me from spiritual envy. Protect me from comparing myself with others. Protect me from dissatisfaction with Your good gifts. Protect me from desiring what others have, whether it is their reputation, their ministry impact, their relationship with You, or any other good thing You have given them. Let me be satisfied with how You have made me and determined to serve You with as much love and devotion as I can, giving You my best rather than wishing for what I don't have.

Gluttony: Lord, protect me from spiritual gluttony. Protect me from consuming more than I need and of failing to concern myself with enabling others to have what they need. Protect me from spiritual selfishness—the temptation to consume rather than contribute, to be served rather than to serve, to be blessed rather than to be a blessing to others.

Wrath: Lord, protect me from spiritual wrath. Do not let my feelings of frustration or irritation or impatience with others prevent me from dealing with them in love. Remind me of Your forgiveness toward me, Your patience with me, and Your forbearance of my immature motives. Remind me of how many advantages and privileges and opportunities You have given me and of the fact that I still remain so far short of Your intentions for me. Help me to love those who fall short just as I love myself, desiring the best for them.

Sloth: Lord, protect me from spiritual sloth. Help me to be a good steward of the opportunities, spiritual gifts, influence, relationships, resources, wisdom, and all the other blessings You have so generously given me. I know I do not deserve any of them. Help me to diligently employ all of them in Your service, for Your glory, and to advance Your Kingdom. Let me not be concerned for my own comfort, ease, convenience, and pleasure, but rather with how to please You and serve others.

I know that all of these "spiritual" sins are expressions of loving You and others inadequately and wrongly. Teach me to love You with all my heart, mind, soul, and strength and to love others as I love myself.

Day 3

Father, thank You for the righteousness I have in Christ. This day and every day I ask that You would advance Your work in me of conforming me to Christ's image. Guide me and enable me to live as He lived, see as He saw, feel as He felt, and serve as He served in His earthly years. Help me remember that I have died to sin so that I might be blind to its distractions and deaf to its voice. Let me live always and only unto You.

Strengthen me in my inner man to live a life of faith, hope, and love—a life of holiness. In love for You and gratitude to You, let me die daily to my selfish desires of laziness and pride. Raise my eyes to gaze upon the eternal realities of Your Kingdom and to do away with lesser things that would distract or deter me in my pursuit of Your will and Your ways. May Your perfect love cast out all fear within me.

I am exceedingly grateful for Your many blessings in my life—family, friends, wealth, and honor. Set a guard on my heart so that I may never idolize these blessings or permit them to usurp Your rightful place in my affections or attention or allegiance. Let me live for You alone. Let me love You with all my heart, mind, soul, and strength and love others as myself. Make me always devoted to You with childlike trust.

May I be a living expression of Your will in all my ways. Let me be a blessing to everyone with whom I come in contact, whether as an encouragement to my brothers and sisters in Christ or as a testimony of Your greatness and glory to those who don't know You. Fill me moment by moment with Your Spirit and with grace so that I might be a fountain of sweet water from which no bitter water ever spills out, no matter how suddenly I may be jarred.

Sailing

Lord, as I sail through this life, continue to serve as my Captain, directing me across the trackless depths to my final port. Though I cannot see beyond the horizon, I trust Your navigation. Though rough and stormy seas beset me, I know You have ordained them to increase my dependence on You, and You control each wave and every wind. Grant me the grace to endure to the end, and may You be glorified in the journey, whether through calm waters or turbulence. Your love is the wind, faith is my sail, and hope is my anchor. All I need is in You.

Day 4

Lord, apart from You I am nothing—less than nothing: dead. I am blind; be my light and my vision. I am ignorant; be my wisdom and my knowledge. I am lost and wandering; be my path and my guide. I am dead; be my life. Let me be dead to sin, evil, and self, but alive to You in every way. Let my life be an expression of Your will and my activities an expression of Your ways.

Make me steadfast and fixed in my focus upon You, no matter how violently storms may surge and blow around me. Let me hear and recognize Your voice no matter how chaotic my situation and surroundings may be. Let me perceive Your works in the situations around me and in the world at large, in big and small ways, so that I may understand Your character and intentions. Let me be instantly directed by Your most subtle glances.

Let me be a joy to Your heart. Let me love and serve and live in such a way that will bring You pleasure and glory. Let me perceive and reflect Your beauty to those around me. Help me spur on Your people to ever greater love and good works. Show me how to redeem the time You give me on the earth. Use me to point others to You and encourage them to know and love You more fully so that You may receive all the honor of which You are worthy.

Journey

Lord, You are the Destination as well as the Path on my journey. You are the Guide. You created the context and You ordain the obstacles. You have prepared everything for Your glory and my good. Enable me to trek with purpose and understanding. Help me assist others on the journey and call those who wander to return to the path. Bring me victoriously to the end with distinction as a guide for others.

Day 5

Lord, be my strength. When I am overcome or overwhelmed by fatigue, or burdens, or sorrows, give me grace to persevere—not in grim resignation, but in gratitude and joy for the ways You can use the situation for my good and Your glory. Give me strength also to resist pleasant and easy things that are not according to Your will for me. Do not let me be distracted or pulled aside by the pursuit of anything other than what You desire for me.

Guide my thoughts and intentions so that I might not be satisfied with choosing between good and evil, but also between the good and the best. Let me find my fulfillment not in comfort and ease and pleasure, but in pleasing You by being and saying and doing nothing else than Your purpose and intention. Let me live for Your pleasure and reputation rather than my own. Let Your life be evident in and through me.

Forgive me when I stray from Your will and Your ways, when by word or deed or thought I pursue my own desires above Yours. Give me courage to deny myself and die to myself.

Teach my heart to praise and thank You in the process because of my faith in Your love for me, a love greater than my love of self; because of my hope of a better reward than anything this world offers; and because of my love for You, for who You are, and for Your worthiness.

Preserve me from finding any joy or pleasure apart from You. Protect me from any satisfaction or fulfillment that comes from advancing my own reputation or power. Let me follow the One who gave Himself to serve others and who sacrificed Himself for their sake and Yours. Give me the humility and perfect obedience that arise from pure love for You and that result in a life of self-giving love for others.

Thank You that although I was Your enemy, You blessed me. You loved me. You treat me not as a slave, even though I am one, and indeed an unworthy one. You treat me as a friend and as Your child. Grow me and mold me until I am a child You are proud of, conformed to the image of Jesus. Lead me safely in joy to Your eternal Kingdom. May I not be concerned as to whether the road is rough or smooth, but only about seeing Your face ever more clearly until that day when I see You face-to-face.

Fragrance

Creator of all things, You have imbued creation with delightful surprises at every turn. Fragrance is an unexpected demonstration of Your beauty. Your inexpressible fullness is perhaps most clearly perceived in the delicate, riotous aroma of sweet, flowering trees and shrubs that envelop us in the spring. Emily Dickinson expressed this sensation when she said, "Inebriate of air am I." Your Spirit endows our existence with this experience. When You were on earth as a man, Your life exuded it. May I be so infused by Your love that I exhibit the same ineffable splendor.

Day 6

Infinite triune God, I cannot comprehend Your greatness. Day by day I ask that You stretch my mind and my imagination so that I may more fully appreciate Your glory and praise Your worthiness.

I cannot imagine You being outside of time, having the ability to see the end from the beginning. I cannot imagine that with You a thousand years are like a day and a day is like a thousand years.

I marvel at the thought that the rise and fall of entire galaxies, empires, individuals, and single-celled organisms are all under Your complete control, awareness, and concern. Such infinite power, knowledge, and presence are incomprehensible to me.

I cannot fathom the vast love You demonstrated in sending Christ to die in order that rebellious man might know You and be transformed and remade in Your image once again, as at creation. Such sacrifice and self-giving are beyond my grasp in either intellect or emotion.

Let such overwhelming realities turn my heart and mind from lesser things. Remind me that my opportunities to respond to Your extravagant gifts are limited in this world, so that I might seize every opportunity to pursue a life that honors You.

Teach me to redeem the time in serving others for their good, that they might praise and worship You. Instruct me how to glorify You to an ever greater degree. Let me live a life that demonstrates Your will and Your ways, in complete dependence upon You.

Music

Lord of all mysteries, I cannot understand the unexpected ways in which music can move and touch us. Melody can move our souls; harmony can lift us up or cause us to mourn. Teach my heart to worship You in ways it can discover only through music. Allow me to magnify and exalt You through heavenly tunes. Show me how to communicate deeply with You in new songs You place within my heart.

You are the conductor. Enable me to play the music You teach me by a life that lives out the music You place within me. May it be a sound that is pleasing to Your ear, and may it draw others to You as the Lord of the choir and the orchestra of the universe.

Day 7

Lord, give me a unity in my life—a unity of thought, desire, emotion, word, and deed. Let that unified being be entirely focused on serving and pleasing You. Forgive me for the times when discord in myself hinders me from being what You intend me to be. Let the life of Christ be fully expressed in me with such harmony that I am perfectly in tune with Your intentions.

Give me a soul and spirit attuned to Your will. Let my only fear be of disappointing You. Let my only hope be for the redemption of all things in Your eternal presence through eternity. Let my only thought be of doing Your will. Let my only love be for You, and from You for others. Let my only desire be to know You more fully so that I might make You more fully known and so that I might more fully love You.

Let my wisdom be of You, my riches in You, my power from You. May I see the emptiness of the false wisdom, riches, and power offered by the world. May all my happiness be from Your image, presence, service, and favor. You are my wisdom, my treasure, and my strength.

Agriculture

Lord, when You created Adam, You placed him in the garden to tend and care for it. Thank You for preserving a vestige of that high calling in farms. Let the lessons of the farm teach me of Your ways in the world. Let me recognize Your orderliness, Your beauty, and the discipline of an unmixed life. As I observe Your cultivation of fields, vines, and trees, may I gain a passion for consistent growth in serving You by blessing others and glorifying You. Show me the power and fulfillment of purpose in the wonder of draft animals as they submit to their masters. Teach me the dignity of blessing others and serving the common good as I observe the hard work and persistence of the farmer. Let me serve You with these same traits as I am pruned by You to achieve Your purposes and to bear much fruit so that You will be glorified.

Day 8

Dear Father, my days are worthless and empty unless they are spent in Your presence, expended in Your service, and used for Your glory. Only by Your grace, strength, wisdom, and enabling can I do anything, including taking my next breath. Grant that I may rely fully on You and not waste Your provisions. Direct me and gently guide me to rely on You every moment, in every word, every step, every thought.

Give me a constant desire to know You and make You known, to give You praise, to demonstrate Your love, and to advance Your Kingdom. Let me be about Your business so as to become an instrument of blessing to all with whom I come in contact. Let me be Your hands and feet and voice in whatever corner of creation you lead me, being used in such a way that Your will is done on earth as it is in heaven.

Government

King of kings, I long for Your perfect rule. You have given us imperfect rulers. They are a shadow of what You intend perfect government to be. Let us learn from them and submit to them as we pursue a corporate achievement of Your purposes in being obedient people and collaborating to bless others as You have blessed us. May their shortcomings be a reminder to us of Your greatness as we long for better things, better laws, and better people.

May we labor for purer expressions of Your will and live lives above and beyond the letter of human law to demonstrate the spirit of Your will. Let us, as Your people, demonstrate love among ourselves and to those outside Your family so that the whole world might see the perfection of our King and submit to Your rule. Let us live by Your Kingdom's laws as You have clearly communicated them in Your commands. Let us serve Your Kingdom's purposes by living in love and seeking the salvation of those outside Your family. Let us use our resources according to Your priorities. Let us prioritize our time and energy for Your purposes. Let us live our lives with an awareness of Your presence so that we might at all times be attentive to the slightest indication of Your intention. You are our King.

Day 9

Gracious Father, source of all that is good, let me be fully satisfied in You, never seeking anything else or satisfied with anything less. Give me a constant dissatisfaction with anything other than Yourself. Let me never confuse the blessings You provide with Yourself, or the gift with the Giver, or the lesser desires I have with the greater things that await me. Conform me more each day to Jesus' life and character, and daily put to death anything that varies from His image.

Let Your will be my delight. Let me live to please only You rather than myself or others. May I rejoice to be counted worthy to suffer for You when others see my faith as foolishness, my meekness as weakness, my zeal as madness, my hope as delusion, and my love for You as insanity. Support me with the hope and strength of heaven as I pursue eternal riches. Let me be known as one who lives always and only for You.

Potter

You are the potter; all creation is the clay. You are working it according to the intention of Your will. I am but a small lump. Thank You for bothering with me at all. I ask that You would make something of exquisite beauty from me that would reflect Your greatness and glory. I know that You must remove many impurities from me to ensure that only fine clay remains. I know that pressure must be exerted on me to shape me. I know that I must face fierce flames to make permanent the shaping You intend. Your pleasure is worth it all. Do what You must. Make me a vessel of use to You and a blessing to others.

Day 10

Lord, Your kindness and grace, which give me life and all spiritual blessings, are the same kindness and grace by which you test, purify, and exercise my faith. Help me receive all Your dealings with me with unmitigated gratitude, whether they be pleasant or unpleasant in the moment. I know that the difficulties You allow are for my good and Your glory as You teach me obedience, perfect me, and allow me to be identified with Christ.

Enlarge my desires and increase my expectancy. Let faith shape my hope so that I might understand Your eternal perspective in shaping me for eternity. Prepare me for eternal service and communion with You. Prepare me not only for the prosperity and adversity I will experience on earth, but even more so for Your eternal purposes in and through me. You are all I need. I love and trust You.

Communicator/Revealer

Lord, thank You that You communicate, and that You are relational in every way. Your creativity is evident in the amazing variety of ways in which You speak. Your creation, Your acts, Your people, Your Word (both living and written), and Your Spirit within us—all these provide continuous evidence of Your character, nature, will, and purpose, as well as Your particular intentions for each one of us.

Tune our hearts to the frequency of Your messages. Give us the sensitivity to recognize Your voice, the faith to act on what we hear, and the wisdom to be transformed by it. Conform us to Your image and will. Thank You that Your Word is powerful and effective, not only in creation but in re-creation.

Enable me to transmit the messages I hear from You to others, so that I might be a conduit of Your blessings. Use me to advance Your Kingdom as a messenger and ambassador of Your glorious magnificence.

Day 11

Lord, let me not shrink back from the second cross, the one I am to bear. Be patient with me as You were with the twelve disciples, recalling as often as necessary that the path to life is through death. Keep me humble, dependent, grateful, and joyful in the process. I want to be as assured as a nursing child with its mother, fully content to be in Your presence. I belong to You. Shape and remake me as You wish.

Truth

You are the Truth. You are the Plumb Line. You are the Standard. You are the Pattern. You are the Ultimate Reality. Draw me to the truth and conform me to it. Let my life be lived in such a way as to demonstrate, advance, and bear witness to Your truth. Give me such a thorough recognition and understanding of the truth that any variance will be detected immediately.

If that variance is within me, enable me to correct it by the work of Your Spirit. If it is in others around me, let me humbly and lovingly deal with it as You direct. If it is in the world, show me how I should respond so that I might be Your instrument to further Your will on earth.

Day 12

Immortal and infinite God, gently teach me to serve You with humble reverence and godly fear. Do not permit me to hide sin in my heart or indulge worldly attitudes or desires. Cleanse me so I might enjoy Your presence. Rule my heart so I might not desire earthly pursuits. Let me be indifferent to earthly possessions, positions, or pursuits. Give me instead a pure and holy desire for Your righteousness and presence.

Produce in me a disposition that recognizes my service to You as perfect freedom. Purge from me all pride, fear, and shame so that I may courageously share Your greatness with everyone and seek an ever more intimate knowledge of Your heart. Fill me with Your wisdom and love. Let me serve others as an expression of my love for You. Infuse me with Your Word and peace that I might be a source of light and encouragement for others.

Power

All power and authority are Yours. You are mighty and strong, even omnipotent. You work all things after the counsel of Your will. I cannot comprehend this, but I praise You for it. I am extremely grateful that Your power is expressed in mercy, grace, justice, kindness, goodness, and love.

When I feel weak and weary, and when I am tempted to lose hope and heart, remind me of Your strength and give me all I need to do Your will. Let my inner person confidently pursue Your path for me without concern for difficulties, knowing that You will carry me through to Your purposes. Let me strengthen others by reminding them of Your mighty power.

Day 13

Father, make me like my elder brother, Jesus. Shine Your light within me and through me. Show me the way You have prepared for me, the path You intend for me to walk. Guard my heart from the enticements of the enemy and the world. I know my heart's weakness and deceit if it is not stayed on You.

Let my lips and my life draw others to greater heights of living in faith and love. May the lazy be spurred on to greater diligence by my example. Let those who are distracted by the pleasures or power of this world be refocused on eternal things by observing my resolute attentiveness. Let those who are timid be emboldened by my encouragement.

Make me a mirror of Your grace to show forth the joy of service. Let my joy in You brighten the hearts of the discouraged. Demonstrate through me how one can perform earthly responsibilities with an eternal perspective. Give me Your heart of compassion for those who are ignorant of You or in misery, that they might experience true love.

Teach me to walk as Jesus walked, to see as He saw, to hear as He heard, to think as He thought, and to perceive Your work in the world around me in both small and large ways. Clothe me each day with His humility so that I may count others as more important than myself and live a life of service to "the least of these" as a sacrifice of love to You.

Authority

Lord, You are sovereign over all creation. You superintend all things for Your glory. You work everything in such a way as to test our hearts, to help us grow into the likeness of Christ, and to teach us to walk by faith. Help us to be quick to learn the lessons You teach and to grow in our understanding and love of You.

You arrange events both large and small to draw people to Yourself, creating dissatisfaction through pain, grief, suffering, and emptiness or demonstrating Your love, kindness, and greatness. Grant those who do not yet know You the faith to respond positively to Your offer of redemption, and send Your children to make the way clear.

Help me to be grateful for all Your works, whether they are pleasant or unpleasant. Guide me to respond well to all situations, whether or not I understand Your reasons for them. Show me Your desires so that I may ask, seek, and knock with bold perseverance to change what You desire to change, and also so that I may patiently and joyfully endure what You desire to maintain. Help me to learn quickly the lessons You teach.

May the nations submit to You, either willingly and humbly or by the exercise of Your activity. May the spiritual forces of darkness be bent to Your purposes, even if unwittingly. May Your Kingdom come and Your will be done on earth as it is in heaven. May Your authority be recognized by all very soon. Come quickly, Lord!

Day 14

Lord, strengthen me to pursue You and know You more fully until You reign supreme in me. Let every thought, word, and deed express Your character from a pure heart full of faith and love. Let me overcome the evil in the world by works that arise from this faith and love. Bind me close to You in heart, mind, soul, and strength.

Show me grace and mercy when I am weak and when I fall. Help me show that same grace to others when they need it. Protect me from the attacks of the enemy by the spiritual armor You provide. Strengthen me for the conflict, and give me endurance for the race You set before me. Let me be victorious by Your power.

My slowness to seize Your provision of these blessings is an expression of my lack of understanding and faith. Increase my faith. Stir holy zeal in me, that I may not hesitate or hold back from Your clear call to advance. Whether I advance or stumble, let me walk humbly, acknowledging my failures in leaving undone what should be done and in doing other than what You intend.

Impress on me deeply that the time is short, the work is great, the responsibility is serious, and eternity is near. May I never forget that You see and hear all things in your sovereignty, so that I may live in a way that pleases You and is aligned with Your will. Continue to work in me until You are constantly the beat of my heart, the center of my thoughts, the ruler of my lips, and the path for my feet.

Faithfulness

Lord, thank You for being the great I AM, the same yesterday, today, and forever. You are the only thing in existence that is completely reliable. We depend on nothing and no one else. You are the foundation and the pinnacle of everything, the source and the end.

Let me never for a moment put my trust, faith, or hope anywhere but in You, that I might not be disappointed or waste my life by investing in anything else. Help me point others to Your absolute trustworthiness. I praise You, for You alone are worthy, my Rock.

Day 15

Lord, do not let me waste Your grace and mercy. Do not let me be a source of shame for You, by either what I do or what I fail to do. Let me serve others in love, for their benefit and Your glory. Let my life bring You joy and be both useful for Your Kingdom and beautiful for Your praise.

Make my life a living demonstration of Your demeanor and attitude in both my words and actions. As I journey on the road You call me to travel, let me be effective in calling others to join me. Let my example be as salt and light to those around me. Let me be an encouragement to love You.

Give me divine light so that I may have wisdom and discernment in all situations. Purify my heart so that I may continually be prepared for life's remaining duties, whether in suffering or in comfort. Prepare me to serve with distinction not only in this life, but even more so in eternity, that I may bring joy to Your heart forever.

Holy Yet Immanent; Distant Yet Near

My exalted and holy Lord, You are completely other—entirely separate from Your creation—yet You have made Yourself available to us. You are absolutely incomprehensible and inaccessible, yet You have made Yourself intimately known to us. In Christ, You have bridged the gap and come near. In the Holy Spirit, You have even entered into us, indwelling us and transforming us.

Words cannot express the wonder of this indescribable gift. I cannot grasp it. I am bewildered and amazed. I marvel. Help me to never lose this astonishment. Capture my constant focus so that I might persist in searching out the astounding mystery of knowing You. Let me transcend my natural perception of life and discern Your supernatural design and activity by which You craft all things after Your purpose and reveal Your character and magnificence.

Use me as Your instrument to increase others' awareness and admiration of Your infinite worthiness. Demonstrate through me a life that is fit for a restored creation, a profound grasp of Your purposes that shapes my daily pursuits. Prepare me for life in the new creation through a deeper walk with You, a more thorough conformity to Your ways, a grander perception of Your purposes, and an increasingly renewed life in Your Kingdom.

Day 16

Lord, by Your Spirit, live in and through me. Let Your breath be my prayers. Inhabit my praises. Speak in my words. Inspire my thoughts. Let my hands do Your work and let my feet take me in Your paths. May Your desires and passions be my heartbeat. Conform me fully to Your image so that I may be an expression of heaven on earth.

Mercy with Justice

Holy God, Your righteousness is absolute. Thank You that You are so pure that no fault or failure can be tolerated in Your presence. Your perfection is absolute. But loving Father, I cannot but be even more grateful for Your mercy. In Your wisdom and love, You have offered an intimate relationship with You to those who will respond to Your gift in Jesus.

We do not deserve it. We never could. You have chosen to sacrifice Yourself to make it possible, to grant us Your purity and perfection. Teach me to live in such a way as to make evident the work You have begun in me. Show me how to bring joy to Your heart in my daily thoughts, words, and actions. Finish the process of conforming me to the image of Christ. Use me to call others to that inestimable adventure as well.

Instruct me how to relate to others with Your same character. Let me be both just and merciful. Allow me to love others sacrificially and so model Your essential nature. Demonstrate in and through me how You intend for life to be lived in Your Kingdom. Let the surprising and even shocking example of this love draw many to You as the author of life and love. Strengthen me to persevere in that life and love despite all the opposition of the enemy.

Day 17

Lord, shape my thoughts and let me see Your activity everywhere. Let me see Your love, not only in the cross and Your church, but also in the world around me, whether in pleasant things or painful and sorrowful ones. Help me recognize Your discipline and training for what they are, an expression of deep love as You equip and prepare Your people for eternity.

Let the sun remind me of the Sun of righteousness whose brightness surpasses it. Let the rain remind me of the showers with which You water my soul. Let streams remind me of the river in the eternal city. May the temporary shadows of beauty in this creation cause my soul to yearn for the eternally solid and indescribably fulfilling new creation you are preparing.

Enable me to continually recognize You more fully so that I may more fully make You known to others. Let me understand You more deeply in order that I may be more fully conformed to Your image. Cause me to discern more constantly Your communications and overtures so that I might respond more attentively.

Trinity

Father, Son, and Holy Spirit, Your eternal unity and relational nature are a revelation. How can complete selflessness combine with such strong identity? How can complementarity be so complete as to be union? How can identity be so clear yet so multifaceted? You are complete, yet You invite Your children to join in Your being, to include us in Your family of One.

Father, You reign over everything as the Source, the Destination, the Author. Son of God, You express the Father so we can comprehend Him. You are the Agent of creation and salvation. You serve the Father in order to bring everything into submission to Him, so that He can in turn place it all under Your authority. Holy Spirit, You indwell us, teach us, and conform us to the image of Christ. You give words to our yearnings and enmesh us into Your being.

Awesome Trinity, guide us, shape us, and incorporate us together with Yourself. Be pleased to work Your love in and through us as Your body, seamlessly expressing Yourself in and through us to one another as an outworking of Your essential nature, and to those outside Your body as a testimony to Your active union in the world. Let our unity be a powerful demonstration of Your preeminence. Your supremacy is worthy of all praise and honor.

Day 18

Father, the more fully I know You, the more I see my shortcomings and failures. I see that even my most noble efforts are tainted by selfish motives. The more I recognize Your power, the more I acknowledge my weakness. The more I understand Your wisdom, the more I see my utter weakness and inability.

Therefore, let me not waste another moment living in the flesh, but rather let me live in the Spirit. Fill me to overflowing. Consume me so that I may not only be focused on Your Kingdom, but to do so in the power of the Holy Spirit. Let me not think of myself or even to be motivated by the enjoyment of service, but rather to delight merely in Your worthiness and Your presence.

Be my wisdom, strength, endurance, faith, hope, love, and every other thing I require to live a life that brings joy to Your heart. Apart from You I can do absolutely nothing. In You I have enough, even if all friends, material things, or manmade organizations fail me, or if creation itself is burning up around me. In fact, in the loss of worldly things, I more truly understand Your worthiness and sufficiency.

I do not have even the faintest imagination of what is needed to dwell and serve in the new heaven and new earth. I trust You to fit me for that marvelous privilege, whatever the cost in this world. Use me also to help in preparing as many others as possible for that purpose as well. May all Your people understand Your ways and purposes so that together we might cooperate with Your work in us.

Omnipresence

Lord, I cannot truly understand how Your presence is constantly in every place. You abide in all the universe, and Your superintendence is evident from the mysteries of subatomic intricacies to the coordination of billions of galaxies. Despite the universality of Your presence, You are intensely personal in Your concern for and involvement with all creation.

I exalt You for this unfathomable infinitude. Show me how to float with utter abandon in the certitude of Your sovereign control and inestimable goodness. Let me be in total synchrony with Your workings and not resist or doubt You in any way. Let my responses be always of pure love and trust. Allow me to communicate Your greatness to others so that they might worship You more truly.

Day 19

Father, I eagerly anticipate the day when there will be no more sorrow, pain, or loss; when no weariness overwhelms, no zeal flags, no sin hinders; when no unbelief, fear, or pride in myself or others causes grief to You and creates a barrier between us; when no distractions derail me from the path You have prepared.

Give me the grace now to live high above these temporal challenges. Let me live a sanctified life with my eyes fixed on You. Let Your love be my consolation, Your glory my joy, Your purposes my pathway, and Your will my resting place. Let every difficulty or setback serve only to increase my hunger to know You more fully and increase my hope, so that I may endure more faithfully.

Omniscience

Lord, You know every detail, seen and unseen, of all creation. Your awareness is constant and complete. You recognize every cause, every effect, every interaction, every relationship. You foresee every response, every possible future. You orchestrate every occurrence and every decision, whether taken in conscious submission to Your will, in opposition to Your will, or in complete unawareness. In Your wisdom You work all things together to accomplish Your purposes.

Instruct me so that I might always be intentional in cooperating with Your desires and not waste my life in seeking my own way. May my thoughts be drawn after Yours. Give me wisdom to perceive Your activity and intentions so that I might steward the pursuits of each day. Allow me to share Your profound discernment and unassailable judgments with others so they might honor You more fully.

Day 20

God who sees the heart, do not let me rest until my heart is blameless before You—not simply in a legal sense, but as a day-to-day expression of my life. Do not let me settle for being born of the Spirit; help me press on to be filled with Him, attentive to His inclinations, and walking in Him.

Let me not be content with professing belief if I am not demonstrating that belief by an obedient life of faith in good works and service. Let my sincerity be demonstrated through horror at the thought of offending You, concern to know Your will, and willingness to deny myself for Your sake.

May nothing within or outside me cause me to grieve You, be blind to Your glory, offend Your children, turn me from Your instructions, or forget Your promises. Do not allow my earthly activities to damage my spiritual life or let my earthly concerns eclipse my spiritual concerns.

Do not permit anything to overshadow the one thing I need—to be in Your presence. Instead, give me a heart that is attentive to You, sensitive to Your guidance, responsive to Your correction, and quick to respond to

Your direction. Teach me the art of abiding in You, so that I might be in the world as Your instrument but not of it.

Purify my heart so that You reign supreme in every thought and motive. Be glorified in me and through me by being my only desire. Allow my pursuit of knowing You to more intimately inspire others to do the same. Let the result be greater glory to You as sinners turn to follow You and saints are drawn to pursue You more intently.

Omnipotence

Lord, the enormity of Your strength is limitless, the enormity of Your power beyond reckoning. Your boundless greatness defies description and Your consummate glory transcends comprehension. Your authority is ineffable and Your rule is unequivocal. Omnipotent God, everything that exists and happens is under Your sovereign control, so that You work all things after the counsel of Your will.

I can rest completely in the knowledge that You are capable and trustworthy to bring about righteous perfection with mercy and love. When I don't see any hope of straightening what has been bent, of restoring what has been twisted, I know You can make all things new.

I do not understand why You choose to limit Yourself by working through weak people, but in Your wisdom You exercise restraint and so demonstrate Your amazing ability to work even through weakness. Develop in me a confidence in Your inscrutable way of showing Your power through frailty. Teach me to be gentle, as You are, patient with those who are struggling. Instruct me in showing meekness and humility to the feeble and compassion to the needy. Thank You for dealing with me in this way, in Your grace and mercy. Help me treat others as You have treated me.

Day 21

Lord, receive the reward of Your suffering. May unfathomable numbers of people submit willingly and joyfully to Your reign. Let Your rule be acknowledged by all and Your will advanced throughout the earth. Use me as You desire in this cause. Whether by my success or suffering, whether by my health or by my illness and pain, whether in my life or death, be glorified. Show me how to labor to this end, and strengthen me to do so. Allow me to play the part You intend in bringing all things into subjection to Your loving authority and power.

Since I am entirely Yours, let me accept with equal joy whatever circumstances You allow, knowing that You can be as greatly glorified in sacrifice as in victory. Give me wisdom to perceive what is from Your hand and what derives from the attacks of the enemy, so that I might not accept any barrier or burden by which he might seek to hinder me. Purify my soul from discouragement, bitterness, or fear by fixing my desires only on You. Give me contentment with Your good gifts.

Show me both what to do and what not to do so that I may invest all the capacity You give me in what is worthy. Give me fulfillment in Your calling and presence. Thank You for the privilege of serving You, but even more for the privilege of being Your child and working with You in this world. Prepare me to serve You well, not only in this world but also in the next, where Your will is expressed in the fully restored perfection of all creation. Create in me now a shadow or an aspect of that condition, as a testimony and trophy of Your grace.

Eternality

Eternal God, I cannot fathom the fact that You are outside time, able to see the end from the beginning. You are the great I AM living in the eternal now. Your victory is already won. Your purpose is already accomplished. You have not only "read the end of the book," but You wrote it.

Teach me to live by faith in the light of eternity. Help me keep my eyes fixed on eternal things and my hope fixed upon them. Tutor me to tune my heart to Your ceaseless praise. Guide me to walk in the reality of Your promises that are not yet visible to my earthly eyes. Grant me the ability to communicate eternal truth to people who are looking merely at temporal realities. Use me as a purveyor of hope and faith to people trapped in the present.

Day 22

Lord of mercy, make me merciful. Let me, like You, prefer to serve the hopeless and downtrodden. Let me bless the homeless, depressed, mentally ill, sin-controlled, hopeless, grieving, and helpless.

Fill my thoughts with ways to demonstrate Your love, to show forth Your kindness, and to serve rather than being served. May many people be drawn to You and glorify Your Name as a result.

Goodness

Dear heavenly Father, I am totally indebted to You for Your goodness, kindness, mercy, compassion, and gentleness. I am unworthy of these blessings and always will be. My only virtue is that You have loved me. I cannot understand that fact, but I will always be grateful for it.

Show me how to imitate You as a doting child imitates a beloved parent. Teach me how to follow Your example in demonstrating Your character. Conform me to the image of Christ. Transform my heart to be fit for eternity with You. Let me bless others as You have blessed me, regardless of the worthiness of the people I love and serve. Because I am limited, show me whom You would have me focus on in showing Your love. Let me not miss any of the good works You have prepared for me to do.

Day 23

Lord, by Your Spirit I ask that You would continually refine and purify my character. Clothe me with humility. Clarify my path moment by moment. Increase my zeal and devotion for You. Cause me to realize the brevity of my earthly stay and order my steps accordingly. Cure me of the foolishness of delay and indecision. Glorify Yourself through me.

Source, Creator, Author

Lord, You are the First Cause. By Your word, You created everything that exists. You are the author of life and salvation. You designed all things. Through sin, we have distorted, broken, and corrupted Your perfect creation. Thank You that You will restore all things in a new creation. We eagerly anticipate that day when Your perfect design will be renewed.

Lord, please continue and complete the good work You have begun in us to prepare us to serve and live and worship in the new creation. We cannot imagine the fulfillment of that vibrant life lived in Your presence when we will finally see You clearly in Your magnificent glory and perceive Your incomprehensible splendor.

We worship You. It is surprising and amazing that You use even the distortions, brokenness, and corruption brought about by sin to prepare, purify, train, equip, and test us. Your wisdom is inscrutable. You bring life out of death, victory out of defeat, strength out of weakness, and glory out of humility.

We trust You. We are clay in Your hands. Mold us. Use us. Thank You!

Day 24

Lord, forgive me for my woefully inadequate worship. Tune my heart to harmonize with the worship offered by the angels, who see You face-to-face. Forgive my wholly inappropriate sense of entitlement. Let me recognize the amazing and undeserved benefits You have already provided and the unimaginable delights You are preparing for me, so that I might rejoice in gratitude for Your generosity.

Protect my heart from distractions through worldly pursuits or anxieties. Flood my entire being with meditations centered on You and Your Kingdom, in order that my life, worship, and soul might be infused with Your essence. Let my food and drink be Your Word and Your voice. Let my faith be my peace as my spirit is knit more fully into Your presence.

Open Hearts, Hands, Homes, Heavens

Lord, You are the One who opens and no one can shut. Please open the hearts of Your people to love what You love, to hate what You hate, and to desire what You desire. Open the hearts of those who do not love You to receive Your love. Give them the faith to respond to Your worthiness with their submission, gratitude, and devotion.

Open the hands of Your people to serve as an expression of Your blessing, grace, mercy, and love. As we have been blessed, let us be a blessing to others. Let our generosity and compassion toward one another be a testimony of unity that brings glory to Your Name. Let our concern and care for the hurting and needy be a demonstration of Your grace that causes people to glorify Your Name. Let our sacrifices of service mirror Your own sacrifice and thus draw people to You.

May our homes be open as places of constant worship and trophies of Your grace. Teach us how to live such lives of hospitality that we might bring respite, fellowship, and support to the souls of those who enter. Let their spirits be refreshed and made to desire more of You when they enter and experience the relationships and fellowship made possible by Your life in us.

Open the heavens to release the benefits of the abundant life to Your family on earth. Let us be conduits of Your blessings. As strangers on the earth, let Your Kingdom culture be modeled in Your people as a strange and wonderful curiosity in this broken world. Help us keep our eyes fixed on the open heavens so that we might always be responsive to Your will and ways. Make us sensitive to Your direction and intention.

Day 25

Glorious Savior, You are my life, hope, joy, peace, treasure, glory, and end. Conform me to Your character, will, and ways so that I might be a tool in Your hands to bless those around me. Send me where You will, guiding my steps and actions to be an instrument of blessing to serve others. Delight in my love.

Let me reflect the heavenly glow so purely that I burn with Your presence, shedding light in the darkness. May I inspire greater dedication in Your children and create a hunger to know You among those who have yet to follow You. Let me be an example that brings honor to Your Name. Advance the work of remaking me in Your image.

Sanctified Senses

Lord, give me new senses to perceive Kingdom realities. You have given me new life. Let me live that life with full engagement each day. Let me not wait until the new heavens and new earth are revealed to experience the fullness of the abundant life.

Give me ears to hear Your voice guiding my ways and speaking to my heart as I navigate through each day. Give me eyes to see Your activity all around me, the needs You desire to meet, and the gaps You intend for me to fill, so that Your will might be accomplished on earth as it is in heaven. Give me a nose that discerns both the aroma of Your work and the stench of the spirit of the world, so that I might always align with You and carry Your sweet fragrance wherever I go. Give me a tongue that desires to feed on Your every word and eschews the deceptive communications of the enemy. Give me a body that feels the impulse of Your pursuits and recognizes the import of Your touch, as You commune with Your church to influence the rest of creation.

Let all these sources of input help me discern Your will with alacrity. May they continually shape my soul and my spirit after Your image and desire. Grant that I may thereby live more and more by faith rather than by my physical senses. At the same time, use my spiritual senses to strengthen my hope for our final redemption. Let me be yielded wholly to a life consumed by Your love and character rather than by lesser concerns for temporary issues. May the obedience of my heart, soul, mind, and strength be expressed in a life submitted entirely to You.

Grant that my existence may therefore result in glory to You and delight to Your heart.

Day 26

Lord, may my walk with You be all-consuming, so all-encompassing that all other interests appear only as faint shadows. May my attention be captured and maintained upon Your concerns. Protect me from self-delusion. Do not let me be religious but unchanged. Do not let me be merely an unworthy oaf but a soldier engaged in advancing Your cause.

Give me an ever-renewing heart, ever learning to sense Your passions. Let my dependence on You be unwavering and my love complete. Let my inner strength be ever-growing, even as my body becomes more frail. Let every setback, pain, grief, and disappointment only serve to increase my yearning to experience Your fullness more comprehensively.

Redemption of Four Relationships: God, Others, Self, Creation

Dearest Lord, thank You that Your redemption is past, present, and future. You have redeemed us, You are redeeming us, and You will ultimately and completely redeem us. Thank You that You are redeeming all of creation, restoring and establishing it as an expression of Your glory and greatness.

Thank You that as part of Your redemption You are restoring all aspects of our relationships; with Yourself, with other people, with our own selves, and with the rest of creation.

- You have made us right with You, not counting our sins against us but instead crediting us with the righteousness of Christ, making us Your beloved children.

- You have broken down the dividing walls between us and other people.

- You have given us a new identity in Christ so that we can love others as well as ourselves.

- You have given us a renewed mandate to manage all creation.

I pray that each day we might advance still further in our recognition and practical living out of these marvelous provisions You have made.

- Let us come boldly before You and live ever in Your presence and under Your direction.

- Let us serve one another and sacrifice for one another as You did for us.

- Let us rest in the contented assurance of our place in Your heart.

- Let us constantly bear in mind Your concerned intention for all creation to bear witness to Your power and wisdom and steward it accordingly.

We yearn for the day when all will be fully and finally perfected in Your presence for all eternity. May the hope of that day strengthen us in the interim and guide our efforts in the days You give us on this earth.

Day 27

Levels of Society

Holy Trinity, we ask that just as You relate within Yourself in all unity and mutual submission and love, may you build that same pattern of relationship to us individually and corporately.

- May our families model Your love and testify to Your nurturing in every aspect of life.
- May our communities be an example of your interdependent concern and cooperation.
- May our cities and towns provide a foretaste of the city of God in the new creation, centered in You and lighted by You.
- May our nations display the light of Your glory in all unity as our lives pulse to the beat of Your heart.
- May our global society be a stage for the knowledge of You to spread as we jointly appreciate Your wisdom in interacting with Your creation.

Five Leverage Points in Society

Lord, You shape the affairs of men in many ways. You have ordained that societies everywhere are impacted by shared patterns of behavior. I ask You to stamp Your influence on the affairs of men by infusing Kingdom principles into the various aspects of shared values and designs in the following systems.

Government: Place people You have prepared into positions of leadership. Give them godly wisdom. Grant them a keen awareness of their inadequacy for the responsibilities before them, and then cause them to turn to You for guidance. Make them champions for the downtrodden. Shape their thoughts and feelings and priorities to be in line with Your own.

Commerce: Let business, trading, and the financial sector be expressions of Your design so that giving might be seen as more blessed than receiving. Let financial systems and patterns be honest and used as a blessing for the distribution of practical needs to everyone. Let prosperity prompt people to honor and thank You for Your kindness and provision rather than lead to pride.

Education: May homes and intact families be the primary venue for the massively important task of educating the young. Let them do so with great love and the care and value that recognize the gravity and influence of the task. Let those serving as teachers in schools or other institutions be guided and strengthened by You as they invest in guiding those whom You place under their care. Let all education point people toward You as the great Teacher.

Communications: Shape the interchange of thoughts and ideas in such a way that people begin to question the gaps between Your will and the state of affairs that currently exists. Give people with control over various communications media a sense of responsibility for impacting society, and steer them to focus on issues that will lead people to pursue Your ways. Grant influence to those who know You, and give them insight in how to glorify You and draw people to You.

Religion: Use both those who claim Your Name and those who claim other allegiances to draw people to Yourself. May those who call themselves Your children give no cause for doubting Your glory or character. Let them be an expression of Your grace, love, and goodness wherever they are, both privately and publicly, individually and corporately. May the falsehood, pretension, and perversions of other religious systems be evident to everyone. Prevent the enemy from blinding people trapped in those systems. Allow them to recognize their plight and escape to You. Guide Your people to rescue them.

Thank You for Your constant concern and engagement in the affairs of men. Draw all men to Yourself in order that You might be honored in all the earth.

Day 28

BLE(E)SS Prayer

Dear Father, Your intention is for the benefit of people, that they might flourish as they experience all the goodness of Your creation and design. We pray for every aspect of life for them.

Body: May their bodies be strong and in good health so that they might serve You with vigor and vitality, as You deserve. Let their well-being be a source of praise and gratitude for Your kindness.

Labor: Give them the tasks that You have created them for. Let them find fulfillment, joy, and effectiveness in the jobs You place before them. Show them how to bring honor to You in how they work.

Economics: Provide for their needs with an abundance that will enable them to give generously to others who are in need. Let them experience the joy of giving. May Your financial blessing on their lives be a cause for praise and appreciation of Your goodness.

(E)motions: Let them feel what You feel. Tune their hearts to Your own. Cause them to rejoice in You and to bring joy to Your heart. Allow them to hurt when Your will is abrogated. Give them the illuminating experience of sharing Your disposition toward all things.

Social: Repair any breach in their relationships. May their connections with other people bring life rather than grief. Let their social interactions draw others to You and encourage them to know and love You more deeply.

Spiritual: Grant them lives that are guided and controlled by Your Spirit. May the strength of their spiritual lives be more than sufficient to the degree that they are overcomers in every aspect of life. May their spiritual affluence overflow to others, beckoning them to You. Prepare them for an eternity with You.

Knowing God: Nature, Purposes, Will, Ways, Thoughts, Heart, Desires

I want to know You. Life is empty and meaningless without You. Life is full and fulfilling in Your presence.

Help me comprehend Your nature. I cannot fathom the infinite, so help me wonder at it. Let me marvel at Your perfection. Help me see You as the measure of all things, the standard by which all things are to be judged and find their meaning.

Help me grasp Your purposes. I cannot imagine Your worthiness, so cause me to understand the multitude of ways by which You make it known. Let me trace Your path as You make Your glory known, so that I might more effectively reflect and proclaim it.

Enable me to discern Your will for me in the situations I encounter and in the settings where You place me. Shape my desires so that they conform to Your own. Let me respond in ways that are in concord with Your intentions, always laboring to see Your will done on earth as it is in heaven.

Teach me Your ways so that I consistently mirror Your character and pursue Your ends in appropriate ways. Let me not miss any turn in the path due to taking my eyes off of You. Let me perceive Your working around me even when it is in unexpected ways.

Reveal Your thoughts to me. I want not only to see Your activity but to comprehend Your thinking so that I might appreciate You more deeply. Deepen my own thinking by exposing me to Yours. Let me begin to anticipate Your work as I begin to trace Your mind.

Cause me to plumb the depths of Your passion for Your glory to be perceived, reflected, and proclaimed through creation, and especially through mankind. Let my heart be shaped by Yours. Let my own emotions be framed by Yours so that I might respond as You would.

Enable me to envision Your desires so that I might be captivated by what delights You. Let me not pursue lesser things than Your intentions. I want my desires to be wholly determined by Yours, for as the loving Creator You know what is best.

Day 29

Responses to and Benefits from Suffering

[This prayer is a summary of the Persecution and Suffering blog post series from 2017, which is one of the files available for free download at obeygc2. com. You can find biblical references for all these requests in that document.]

Lord, I want to respond well to difficulties You allow into my life. Please help me by Your Spirit to delight and glorify You and to grow in my own faithfulness and maturity by doing these things when faced by unpleasant circumstances:

Think about Your perspective on it;	Worship You;
Wait for You and rely on You for relief;	Call out to You;
Hope in You and seek You;	Not fear;
Quietly submit to You;	Mourn;
Humbly respond to You and to the human agents;	Commit my life to service even in difficulty;
Not grumble or complain;	Avoid distractions from Kingdom purposes;
Examine my life;	Seek to please You in the midst of it;

Act righteously, even when it will result in persecution;

Rejoice greatly;

Be glad;

Not resist evil people acting against me;

Love my enemies;

Pray for those who persecute me;

Love You more than anyone, including family members;

Count You as more important than anything in life;

Be willing to sacrifice everything for You;

Deny my own will and desires and serve Your purposes daily;

Not be selfish or conceited;

Humbly consider others as more important than myself and serve their interests;

Not use my position to my advantage but rather to serve others;

Humble myself by being willing to suffer for the benefit of others;

Be encouraged;

Continue proclaiming the good news of Jesus publicly and privately;

Continue teaching others about the Kingdom life publicly and privately;

Promote the Kingdom wherever I go;

Welcome instruction about the Kingdom even when it leads to suffering;

Model service in the midst of suffering for other believers;

Imitate followers of Christ who suffer well for serving You;

Persevere, demonstrate faith, and endure;

Be filled with the Spirit;

View the trials as identification with You and for Your sake;

Continue to speak the truths of the Kingdom that I have believed;

Not lose heart;

Fix my eyes on unseen and eternal realities rather than my present situation;

Not cause others to stumble;

Show great endurance through every kind of unpleasant circumstance and situation;

Live out purity, understanding, patience, and kindness;

Demonstrate a Spirit-filled life of sincere love, truthful speech, and godly power;

Show forth righteous living in spiritual warfare in the face of any response;

Be content with being considered false, being beaten, poor, sorrowful, and dying;

Work hard for the Kingdom;

Be willing to face every kind of difficulty, danger, discomfort, and sorrow;

Be concerned for the welfare of others;

Boast in my weakness;

Delight in weaknesses, insults, hardships, persecutions, and difficulties;

Glory in my sufferings;

Share in Your sufferings;

Consider myself a sheep to be slaughtered and sacrificed;

Be willing to lose my freedom;

Count any and every earthly thing as a loss compared to knowing Christ;

Participate in Your suffering and death willingly;

Intentionally suffer through self-discipline as a sacrifice of service;

Seek to please You;

Consider my service and sacrifice as the least I can do for You;

Die to self with You;

Persevere;

Practice Your commands;

Serve as Your ambassador and represent Your desires and ways to others;

Fervently pray with cries and tears to You for relief;

Reverently submit to You;

Remember Your faithfulness in past suffering;

Stand with others who are suffering and join them in it;

Joyfully accept the confiscation of my property;

Live by faith;

Not shrink back from serving or speaking for You;

Choose to be mistreated with Your people rather than hiding my heavenly citizenship in order to escape;

Value Your treasures more than the treasures of this world;

Embrace any sacrifice You call on me to make;

Love God with all my heart, soul, mind, and strength;

Keep Your commands;

Welcome and choose every form of opposition and pain and discomfort for Your sake;

Resist and struggle against sin, even to death;

Not make light of discipline;

Not lose heart;

Endure hardship, knowing its benefits;

Respect You and submit to You;

Consider it pure joy;

Let endurance have its full result;

Be patient and persevere;

Bear up under unjust suffering;

Patiently endure unjust suffering;

Not commit sin or deceive to escape hardship;

Not lash out at those causing me pain;

Not threaten;

Entrust myself to You, knowing You will judge righteously;

Not fear threats or be frightened;

Revere You as Lord;

Be prepared to give a witness for my hope, with gentleness and respect;

Arm myself with the purpose to suffer as You did and with Your attitude;

Not be surprised at fiery ordeals and tests because they are expected and normal;

Rejoice at the opportunity to share in Your sufferings;

Be alert and of sober mind;

Resist the devil, firm in my faith;

Be aware that believers around the world are suffering for their faith;

Not be afraid of future suffering; and

Be faithful to the point of death.

As I do respond in this fashion, I ask that You will, in and through the suffering:

Position me to bless others;

Test, refine, and prove me and my faith;

Give me hope;

Show me Your love is unstoppable and You are good and all I need;

Show me You are listening and are near;

Bless me;

Comfort me;

Equip me to comfort others;

Prepare me to inherit the Kingdom of heaven;

Increase my reward in heaven;

Discover my true and real life in You;

Help me know You more intimately;

Help me become more like You and identify with You more fully;

Help me gain more of Your character;

Demonstrate the permanence and power of Your love for me;

Save my life in You;

Cause me to bear more fruit;

Teach me peace;

Teach me to hope in my future eternal comfort and blessing;

Demonstrate Your trust in me and honor of me;

Give me joy;

Announce Your message broadly;

Encourage others in their faith;

Show love to my brothers and sisters in the faith;

Show my worthiness of the Kingdom;

Make room for Your justice;

Show Your power in me;

Demonstrate Your life in me;

Foreshadow my future glorification (as in Your resurrection);

Cause others to be drawn to You;

Result in thanksgiving from others for my sacrificial ministry;

Renew me day by day through Yourself;

Bestow eternal rewards;

Prove my genuineness;

Validate my ministry;

Validate my words;

Make my life known;

Enrich the lives of others;

Show where my true riches are, where my heart is;

Keep me humble;

Give me perseverance, godly character, and hope;

Honor me;

Show that I am Your child and heir of Your glory;

Demonstrate my conquering life in You;

Advance the gospel;

Give confidence to fellow believers;

Demonstrate my faith in You, which is my righteousness;

Show me the power of Your resurrection, and help me share in it;

Provide access to Your life and help me reign with You in eternity;

Give me strength to stand;

Crown me with glory and honor;

Perfect me;

Teach me obedience;

Be especially attentive to my prayers;

Enable me to experience better and lasting possessions;

Provide a pathway to receive Your promises;

Be the way of salvation;

Show that the world is not worthy, but You are;

Provide an opportunity for amazing victories that will glorify You;

Teach me discipline;

Deepen my holiness;

Produce a harvest of righteousness and peace in my life;

Produce endurance, perfect me, and make me complete in You;

Enable You to demonstrate Your compassion and mercy;

Prove the genuineness of my faith;

Bring the result of praise, glory, and honor to You;

Help me find favor with You;

Fulfill my calling;

Bring the enemies of the Kingdom to shame;

Keep me free from sin's allure;

Cause me to live more fully for Your will and desires;

Increase my future joy;

Increase Your glory in my life and the fullness of the Holy Spirit;

Bring to pass my restoration, strengthening, firmness, and steadfastness;

Enable me to receive the victor's crown; and

Achieve Your good purposes in my life.

These things can happen only by Your mercy and grace. Thank You for Your mercy and grace!

Day 30

Listening, Perception, Attentiveness

Lord, give me the divinely empowered ability to maintain my focus on You so fully that I will not miss the slightest cue of Your intention. Let my attentiveness be sensitive and unshakable. Allow me to perceive Your slightest glance or gesture. Permit me to pick out Your slightest whisper even in the midst of hubbub and confusion. Tune my spiritual senses to discern and even anticipate Your activity around me, and give me the wisdom to grasp Your guidance for my responses moment by moment. Thank You for Your constant concern with every detail of life.

Homesickness (*Maranatha!*)

Father, I join all creation in yearning for the completion of Your redemption. I ache for the fulfillment of the new creation. I crave the perfection of my new body. I hunger and thirst for the day I will see You fully, face-to-face, in all Your glory. I pine for the renewal of all relationships. I long for the permanent and visceral awareness of Your presence to light the eternal day. My deepest desire is for Your glorious return. Come soon! *Maranatha!*

APPENDIX 2: SONGS THAT ADDRESS THEMES RELATED TO THEOPRAXY

Introduction

Many Christians struggle to express themselves in prayer. They don't know what to say, or they fear that they may not be approaching God properly. Of course, God delights in any communication from a heart that is solely focused on Him. But just as the disciples asked Jesus, "Teach us to pray," many believers today could benefit from having prayer modeled to them.

Many of the great songs of the church, both old and new, are essentially prayers that express our commitment to God and ask for His help, guidance, and inspiration. We sing these songs in corporate or private worship, but most of us rarely draw on them in our own prayers (although if you start using Dick Eastman's prayer wheel, that may change, since five of the sixty minutes are reserved for singing).

In this section of my book, I have collected a very partial selection of songs that I hope will strengthen your prayer life. These hymns and praise songs capture key themes of living a life of Theopraxy. This is an extremely incomplete collection, but serves as an illustrative sampling of what exists.

Due to copyright restrictions, I will simply hyperlink to the lyrics of these songs in the ebook version. If you are reading a printed copy of this book, you may want to download an ebook version to access these lyrics or do an Internet search for them.

"Lord, Speak to Me That I May Speak,"
by Frances R. Havergal

"Open My Eyes, That I May See,"
by Clara H. Scott

"Savior, Teach Me, Day by Day,"
by Jane Eliza Leeson

"Trust and Obey,"
by John H. Sammis

"Wherever He Leads I'll Go,"
by B. B. McKinney

"Living for Jesus," (verse 1 and refrain)
by Thomas O. Chisholm

"Jesus, I My Cross Have Taken,"
by Henry Francis Lyte

"Be Thou My Vision,"
by Ian Lynn

"Blessed Assurance,"
by Fanny Crosby

"Have Thine Own Way, Lord,"
by Adelaide A. Pollard

"I Surrender All,"
  by Judson W. Van De Venter

"In Christ Alone," (verses 1, 4)
  by Keith Getty
  and Stuart Townend

"Take My Life and Let It Be,"
  by Frances Ridley Havergal

"Turn Your Eyes Upon Jesus,"
  by Helen Howarth Lemmel

"Do Everything,"
  by Steven Curtis Chapman

"Live Like That,"
  by Sidewalk Prophets

"Keep Making Me,"
  by Sidewalk Prophets

"Thrive,"
  by Casting Crowns

"So Will I,"
  by Hillsong United

"Every Time I Breathe,"
  by Big Daddy Weave

"All In," (portions)
  by Matthew West

"Everything,"
  by TobyMac

"You're Worthy of My Praise,"
  by Jeremy Camp

"As the Deer,"
  by The Maranatha Singers

"Be Glorified,"
  by Chris Tomlin

"Breathe,"
  by Jonny Diaz

"Draw Me Close,"
  by Michael W. Smith

"Every Move I Make,"
  by David Crowder Band

"Holiness,"
  by Micah Stampley

"I Give You My Heart,"
  by Hillsong Worship

"In the Secret,"
  by Andy Park

"Jesus Lover of My Soul,"
  by Paul Oakley

"Knowing You,"
  by Graham Kendrick

"Lord Reign in Me,"
  by Brenton Brown

"One Pure and Holy Passion,"
  by Passion Conferences

"Step by Step,"
  by New Kids On The Block

"The Potter's Hand,"
  by Hillsong Worship

"When I Look Into Your Holiness,"
  by Kent Henry

"Whatever You Ask,"
  by Steve Camp

"Better Is One Day,"
  by Matt Redman

"I Will Worship,"
  by David Ruis

"Refiner's Fire,"
  by Brian Doerksen

"My Life Is in You, Lord,"
  by Daniel Gardner

I will close this appendix with an ancient prayer song that magnificently describes the Theopraxic life:

Prayer of St. Patrick

As I arise today,
may the strength of God pilot me,
the power of God uphold me,
the wisdom of God guide me.
May the eye of God look before me,
the ear of God hear me,
the word of God speak for me.
May the hand of God protect me,
the way of God lie before me,
the shield of God defend me,
the host of God save me.
May Christ shield me today.
Christ with me, Christ before me,
Christ behind me,
Christ in me, Christ beneath me,
Christ above me,
Christ on my right, Christ on my left,
Christ when I lie down, Christ when I sit,
Christ when I stand,
Christ in the heart of everyone who thinks of me,
Christ in the mouth of everyone who speaks of me,
Christ in every eye that sees me,
Christ in every ear that hears me.
Amen

APPENDIX 3: WRITING POETRY

One practice I find helpful is to compose poetry about what the Lord seems to be emphasizing to me. Poetry is by its nature a limiting form of expression. I find that it forces me to think deeply as I search for just the right word to convey the nuance I am contemplating. It gives me an appreciation for how an infinite God limits Himself in order to communicate to and work through human beings. It also focuses deep thought and clarity because of the strict limitations. And it fosters humility by highlighting our inadequacies of expression.

Suppose, for example, that I decide to write an English sonnet about the Trinity. (You may recall that a sonnet consists of fourteen lines—three quatrains of four lines each and a concluding couplet.) The first quatrain could be about the Father, the second about the Son, and the third about the Holy Spirit, with the couplet expressing a summary statement about the entire Trinity.

Sometimes I find it helpful to construct sets of poems. For example, I have written poems on every section of the Sermon on the Mount and on every parable. In the future, I hope to write a poem on every book of the Bible. The length of the poems ranges widely, from haiku to longer poems of multiple stanzas.

Sometimes I set the poetry to music. Because I am not musically inclined, I look at the metrical index in an old hymnal and choose a hymn tune with the meter (i.e., number of syllables per line) that matches my poem. Or I do the opposite—I select a tune I like and then write a poem with the same meter.

Following is an example—a poem on the virtues of faith, hope, and love, written in long meter (eight syllables per line in iambic tetrameter, with a rhyme scheme of ABAB). There are many great tunes in that meter, so I have listed four possibilities. You could probably write something like this in ten minutes (remember, it's for your own inspiration initially, not for publication), so this need not be a laborious process.

Faith, Hope, and Love

By faith we base our daily walk
Upon the things we cannot see.
Eternal things control the clock.
We live our lives abundantly.

In hope we daily overcome
The challenges that come our way,
Receiving comfort as we plumb
The promise of that coming day.

Through love we live as God commands,
With all our heart and all our soul;
In gratitude, for from His Hand
We have received our lives made whole.

[To the same tune as "I Heard the Bells on Christmas Day" (Waltham) or
"When I Survey the Wondrous Cross" (Hamburg) or "O Master, Let Me
Walk with Thee" (Maryton) or "The Gift of Love" (Hal H. Hopson).]